Rudolf C. Heredia is an independent writer/researcher. He has his doctorate in Sociology from the University of Chicago (1979), and taught sociology at St Xavier's College, Mumbai, where he was the founder Director of the Social Science Centre. From 1990 to 1992, he was Director, department of research, at the Indian Social Institute and edited the institute's journal, *Social Action*, from 1990 to 1993 and again from 2005 to 2008. From 2004 to 2010 he was a research fellow at the Indian Social Institute, New Delhi, and research consultant from 2016 to 2020.

Some of his earlier publications are *Voluntary Action and Development: Towards a Praxis for Non-Government Agencies* (Concept. New Delhi, 1988); *Tribal Education for Community Development: A Study of Schooling in the Talasari Mission Area* (Concept. New Delhi, 1992); *Urban Housing and Voluntary Agencies: Case Studies in Bombay* (Institute of Social Sciences. New Delhi, 1989); *Tribal Identity and Minority Status: The Kathkari Nomads in Transition* (1994). The more recent publications include *Changing Gods: Rethinking Conversion in India* (Penguin. New Delhi, 2007); *Taking Sides: Reservations Quotas and Minority Rights* (Penguin. India, 2012); *Reconciling Difference: Collective Violence in India* (Speaking Tiger. New Delhi, 2021).

He has been residing in Mumbai since October 2020.

A CLOWN FOR GOD, A CLOWN FOR OTHERS

Recollections of an Indian Jesuit

Rudolf C. Heredia

SPEAKING TIGER

SPEAKING TIGER BOOKS LLP
125A, Ground Floor, Shahpur Jat, near Asiad Village,
New Delhi 110049

First published by Speaking Tiger Books 2022

ISBN: 978-93-5447-188-9
eISBN: 978-93-5447-196-4

10 9 8 7 6 5 4 3 2 1

Typeset in Bembo Std by SÜRYA, New Delhi
Printed at Chaman Enterprises, New Delhi

CONTENTS

A BEGINNING

Memory is always selective and mostly self-serving. It adds up to a presentation of one's self that attempts to ease the tensions and contradictions that we all must live through in our lives. So here's where I'm coming from, how far I've gotten and where I might go.

My family hailed from the tiny island of Divar (6x3 kms) in the Mandovi River, 10 kms from Panjim, opposite Old Goa which was once the capital of the Portuguese Province of the East. Our ancestral home is still maintained in the hamlet of Goltim in the village of Navelim, now put into the 'Primero Vado' by the Post Office. But the area is better known as the parish of Piedade (Our Lady of Piety), with its church on the hill. Earlier, there were many chapels and even before that numerous temples, some still standing and new ones coming up. The second parish on the island is San Mathias (St Mathias) also on a hill, but a lower one. Inevitably there is an endless rivalry between the two parishes.

Flat lowlands, called kazan lands, cover the space between hill slopes and river. They have a traditional interlocking system to control the flooding, the holding and releasing of tidal and rain waters, with fixed exits restrained by floating beams. Divar is connected to the mainland by flat-bottomed roll-on-roll-off ferry boats at three points: on Divar's south side, the oldest and shortest route to Old Goa that continues to be the main one; further down the river towards Panjim, there is another that crosses over to Ribandar; and one more at Narva, connecting the island to North Goa. Both these came much later. Electricity came only in 1973 and drove away the ghosts and the romance that came with candlelight and kerosene lamps at home and 'hurricane lanterns' and burning touches on the roads outside.

The bunderaon, the feast of the flags—traditionally held to mark the village boundaries at harvest time—is still enacted in Divar with mock battles, complete with the planting and removing of flags, and finally concluding with an amicable settlement. Divar has now become a tourist attraction as it is one of the few places where the bunderaon is still held. As a Divarkar, I have always felt special and proud to come from 'the most beautiful island in the world'. But those who haven't been there, how would they know!

Our family were landless gentry, 'gaunkars', as were many other Divarkars who had to look beyond the ferry for a living. Of my three grand-uncles, one migrated to Portugal and lost touch with the other two brothers; another joined the seminary and ended up as a canon in the cathedral—the Se, the seat of the Archbishop, officially the Patriarch of the East—an empty title now but once treasured by the Church in Goa. The Se, as with most other national heritage churches of Old

Goa, is now maintained by the Archaeological Survey of India, an agency of the Indian Union Government.

My paternal grandfather, Manoel Augustinho de Heredia (1871–1937), put himself through medical college in Panjim by giving Latin tuitions. He went on to become the government-appointed doctor on the neighbouring island of Chorao. But he became *persona non grata* with the colonial government for his involvement with anti-Portuguese movements and people. He had to leave Goa in a great hurry to avoid arrest. Family legend tells of how he had to be carried over the river in a basket and smuggled out of Goa through Sawantwadi to the north of Goa.

He set up practice in the south of the island city of Bombay, in Kalbadevi, 'little Goa' as the area was known to Goans. The neighbourhood was cosmopolitan though, with new migrants pouring in to make their future in a growing, bustling, industrial-commercial, city-port. Bombay became the Gateway to India, the '*urbs prima in Indis*' (the first city of India), after the opening of the Suez Canal in 1869.

My grandfather's successful medical practice helped him venture into the business world of his Gujarati patients. Besides these professional demands, he and his wife, Angela Mericia de Rocha Herediá (1882-1962), who loved music, enjoyed dancing—especially the quadrilles (a pair of couples in a traditional ballroom dance)—were prominent on the social circuit, for in their home was 'prized laughter and the love of friends'.

Family legend has it that Manoel was a very

good but absent-minded doctor. While he treated his patients, his compounder dealt with the monies. Once when the compounder was too ill to serve at the clinic, my grandmother had to stand-in. She found the daily take had greatly increased. So she asked her husband if the number of patients had suddenly increased. She was told they were about the same as other days. She immediately realized what was happening and the compounder lost his job.

With his business partners, Dr Manoel Heredia was successful in setting up the Asian Life Insurance Company in the new business district of Ballard Estate. This four-storeyed building called—rather unimaginatively—Asian Building, was well located on Nicol Road (now Kamani Marg). The street was lined with a row of laburnum trees that flowered into a golden chain all down the road when in bloom. The family occupied the top floor, the Company the two below, the others were rented out. When my grandfather passed away in 1937, aged sixty-six, the company was up and running. As the eldest son, my father, who was just twenty-nine years old at the time, had to take over his father's responsibilities, both commercial and familial.

My earliest memory of the place is of me yelling my lungs out in protest at being given a bath in my baby tub, though I can't remember why I was making so much noise. Was the water too hot or too cold? I suppose all the sound and fury was just to make my presence felt lest I be thrown out with the bath water. In a large extended family, you got noticed mostly when something went wrong. My elder brother Christopher, nicknamed Kit, was often unwell, so he got lots of attention. I had to do something to get my share. Since I found it was easier to be noticed when you were naughty, I became a mischievous little twit. But soon I came to realize this had diminishing returns and the attention I drew was not always the kind I wanted. However, in a household of many and diverse adults there were many buffers for the rebuffs that every child experiences or imagines. Nuclear families today do not have this safety net.

Angela and Manoel had eight daughters and three sons. Dr Manoel Heredia's Gujarati patients would sympathize with him: 'Poor, Dr Heredia! What will he do with eight daughters?' And his reply would be: 'My eight daughters are my eight treasures.' And they were, because he educated them all. However, he did not hesitate to take two—or was it three?—of them out of college to make a suitable marriage if one could be found. (One was even studying to be a doctor but marriage trumped medicine. Luckily her elder sister married another doctor only after she graduated in medicine with an MBBS herself.)

By the time I came on the scene in 1941, my father, James Nathaniel, was responsible for his mother, Angela de Rocha Heredia; his recently widowed eldest sister, Florinda Correa and her four children, two daughters and two sons, whom my grandfather had brought from Secunderabad to live with us. The youngest was posthumously born and grew up to be Charles Correa, the architect. The next three older sisters—Olga Saldana, Elizabeth Coreia-Afonso and Eleanor Lobo—were all married and lived with families on their own.

Albert, the younger brother, was already a practising medical doctor, married and living with his wife and baby daughter in the neighbourhood, while the youngest brother, Frederick, had gone off to the war. 'There was nothing else for a young man to do at the time,' he told me much later. I still have imprinted in my memory a picture of him on his return: his toothbrush moustache sticking out at right-angles, and slapping down his army major's cap on the dinner table, surprising everyone as he burst through the door, a soldier in uniform coming home unannounced on being decommissioned after the war. His mother was in tears, his three younger sisters hanging on his neck, crying.

I was so proud to have uncle Frederick as my 'padrinho' (godfather), a soldier, big and strong, who at the time seemed far better than my brother's 'padrinho', a mere priest, slim but tall! Then no one thought he might become the Cardinal Archbishop of Bombay later one day. For a brief while, uncle Freddy, as he was called, joined his older brother in the insurance company, but found it too 'boring'. He soon left home again to make a career in the newly formed Indian Administrative Service (IAS).

There were yet three younger unmarried sisters

still in college who lived with us—Angela, Tessa, and Margot. When my father married and brought his wife Irene home (Anna Signorina Scholastica Irena D'Silva, who always insisted she was a 'D'Silva' not a 'Heredia'), they added three more children to the household. Besides, there were three live-in domestic helpers, a cook, a butler and a maid. No wonder I had to make my presence felt lest I'd be lost in the crowd. In retrospect, I believe, it was the numbers we had and the space we gave each other that made for a happy diverse family.

TRANSITION AND INTEGRATION

My mother Irene had read English at St Xavier's College and in 1937, she topped the BA examinations in English Literature. She won the Duke of Edinburgh scholarship, as it was called pre-Independence (it is now called the President's Gold Medal), for being ranked first in a subject that rotated each year. But there was a rider: the winner had to go on to do an MA in the subject. If she were to marry my father it would mean giving up on her post-graduate education. However, in the uncertainties of the 1930s, marriage seemed the more sensible option. From her eldest brother, Anthony, I learnt how she resisted and cried over having to choose between Mrs Heredia, BA and Irene D'Silva, MA. I don't think it was love at first sight, but certainly, love in hindsight.

She herself came from a large family; the only and much-loved daughter, youngest in a house with five elder brothers and a twice-widowed mother. Her integration into another family, one where the male to female ratio was reversed, would have been traumatic but for the unyielding support of her mother-in-law. When as a young bride, Irene crossed the threshold of her new home, one of the first things her mother-in-law did was to entrust the keys of the kitchen and storeroom to her. It was a symbolic gesture of enormous importance, setting the female hierarchy firmly in place, and making for a smooth transition for her and a happy family for all.

Did Irene ever have regrets? It is likely that she did for she was a woman of many talents. But she also had a capacity for love and James Nathaniel was a very good husband, for those times.

I once made bold to ask her: 'Mum, you write so well, why didn't you write more?'

She ruefully answered: 'There were five of you and your *father* was always so busy.'

Surprised, I said, 'Really?'

'Yes,' she really replied. 'Your father was a real MCP but in those days all men were like that.

Stunned, I interjected: 'You know what that means, Mum?'

'Of course, male chauvinist pig,' she said quite nonchalantly.

Yet on the spur of the moment, she wrote an obituary card for her husband of thirty-five years:

will i remember you?
will i remember
your tender smile,
the kindness, the care, the love you showered on me?
it empties my mind
of everything
but you.

(Irene Heredia, 9 April 1975)

Years later, she reminisced about her late husband for a family memoir, which she entitled: 'Here Was a Man'. It was so movingly written precisely because she was not unaware of 'his faults and foibles…an irascibility with those closest to him, mainly his wife….But it was all really due to his essential hypertension which afflicted him all his life. In the few weeks before he died, he seemed to be in an unusually pensive mood. Suddenly one morning of a clear blue sky, without anything leading up to it, he announced to me, "You have been the most beautiful thing in my life!" This from a man never given to extravagant language nor maudlin sentiment… I realized afterwards that it was really a farewell.' This summed up the thirty-five years of her happy, vibrant and fulfilling marriage. Its memories carried her through thirty-eight years of her gracious and grace-filled widowhood.

Decades later, she was to write a short story about 'The Girl Child'; now it's part of the unfinished business she left behind. Perhaps one of her three daughters, or more likely one of her four granddaughters, or more likely eight great-grand daughters, will complete the task in her memory. However, she did complete her memoir in her ninetieth year, *It's Been a Long Day*, spanning two centuries (Goa 1556, 2012).

HOSPITAL EXCHANGE?

My younger sister Chantal was due when I was just four years old. I was told 'she' had to be picked up from the hospital. So when Kit and I were taken to see 'our' baby sister, I was surprised to see that all the babies in the nursery looked similar and more so when all were wrapped up in exactly the same way.

A bit shaken, I asked, 'How do we know which baby is *our* baby?'

I was told: 'Mothers always know.'

That didn't convince me since I couldn't tell the difference myself. When I was particularly naughty, I would be told: 'You must have been exchanged in hospital. No one in our family could be as naughty as you.' Then the doubts only resurfaced and deepened. One day some visiting relatives noticed me and said, 'The boy looks so much like Jimmy,' and all the others agreed. Then at last I finally felt happy and proud to belong. But it only made me more rather than less of a mischievous little imp, and truth to tell, I quite liked the role.

TESTED BY FIRE

An event stamped in my memory is the night of 14 December 1947. That night a fire engulfed Asian Building and took with it everything except the clothes we were wearing. But no one was hurt. That was because of my dad's presence of mind. He sized up the dangerous situation and stuffed us all—fifteen members of the family—in a lift meant for five. My mother was carrying baby Chantal who was playing with flowers—she was mad about flowers, 'paampaam' she called them—oblivious to the mortal danger we all were in. Dad and our man Friday ran down the back staircase as the smoke and flames choked up the front one.

The firemen cleared the street and helped us to safety into the lobby of the Indian Merchants' Chambers opposite and closed the collapsible gate to the entrance lest the flying debris from the burning building injure someone. From that lobby, I could see the mounting flames licking their way up the wooden staircase and finally consume what till then had been home and all I had. I could hear people hysterically asking: 'Is there anyone left behind? Are we all safe?' We were extremely fortunate there was no loss of life. But that was only confirmed hours later as the fire smouldered through the night.

The next morning my dad returned to the scene to find only cinders. It was a trauma that divided our whole family life into pre- and post-'The Fire'. We children were spared the trauma, for we hardly realized the implications of what had happened. We were all divided up and farmed out across our extended family in the city. We children were only too happy to be with our cousins, grateful we were all still there. I remember reading about all this in the next morning's newspapers and feeling so important, because an event I was actually involved in had been reported in the headlines. But the aunts were inconsolable. They couldn't stop crying. My grandmother, the matriarch, determined this had to stop. She had experienced many losses and recoveries in her life and she knew this wouldn't be the last of either.

One day, she exercised her matriarchal authority and called together all the aunts and said: 'Now listen. We had too much. God took it away. No more crying. We start again.'

She had no time for such tears, even while my dad went about stoically putting together a new life for those dependent on him. The old Asian Building passed into history, and the new one was born. 'The Fire' marked the end of a family saga and the beginning of a new one with only our immediate family left in the renovated family nest.

There were five of us. First came Christopher, Kit. I followed next and then came Chantal, and soon after Delia, (nicknamed 'fire baby' because she came after 'The Fire') and last but not least, Daddy's darling, Selena. Actually, I was almost named Adolf, because my padrinho, uncle Freddy who fought in the War had a great regard for German efficiency.

I haven't got over the trauma of 'the Fire', which but for the grace of God almost took us all. Whenever I hear the fire engine's bell ringing in the street, I still go a bit weak in the knees, and one of the first things I do on entering new premises is look for the fire escape.

COMINGS AND GOINGS

We have different ways of coping with tragedies and traumas, the ups and downs of our lives. A clown does it with humour and wit, compassion and empathy. That's why clowns are both funny and sad, as also sunny and mad; children love them, adults respect them even when they can't imitate them; the old at times often regret they didn't give more space to their inner clown. Indeed, it is difficult to be cruel to a clown and so the mask of the clown becomes a form of self-protection for the vulnerable.

I don't think I chose to be a clown, it just seemed to happen naturally along the way. I believe it was my way of coping, a way of concealing my own tears and fears and those of so many others that lie hidden and 'uncried', still damned within one's soul; the *lacrimae rerum* (the tears of things) of Virgil, though mine seem always to be tinged with a touch of humour and mischief.

THE DEAL MAKER

James Nathaniel Heredia often described the life insurance business as the art of taking calculated risks; it has come to be called the art of making deals. He would tell us that his business was to make bets with people that they would live longer than they expected and eventually pay more in premium than they got back in coverage. I suppose he needed a sense of humour as large as the risk to cope with the fallout when the calculations misfired.

He was known in the business world for his honesty and integrity. He would say, 'I may not have much cash but my credit is good!' At home, he was known to be a big tease. Once he said to me with a completely straight face: 'Someone has offered to buy you for a hundred rupees. Should we accept or reject the offer?' It must have been said to put an end to the endless squabbling rivalry between Kit and me.

This had me worried for a while, even though I intuitively knew he had to be kidding. But one hundred was a large number for a child who had just learnt to count, so I proposed a naughty counter deal: 'Take the offer,' I said. 'I'll go and then I'll sneak back home. You can have the money and me.'

Dad sighed at this and said, 'I think *we* would have to pay someone to keep a child as mischievous as you.' So now I felt secure at home and confirmed in my naughtiness. Though I didn't realize at the time, this was my first experience of a win-win situation, which only a genuine clown could have come up with.

LOST AND FOUND

On my first day at school, just six years old, my mother dropped Kit and I off in the kindergarten school at the Fort Convent and introduced me to the teacher. But after my mother left, I looked around and noticed her absence. I panicked and sneaked out into the open street in search of her. But it was quite deserted. Fortunately, the watchman of the adjoining church, the Holy Name Pro-Cathedral, had seen me with my mother when we had visited there earlier that morning and he took me to her. Mum thought my school's kindergarten classes were over and brought me straight home. There was panic in the school when I was found to be missing, until a telephone call confirmed that I was home, safe and dry.

The next day I was made to sit with my elder brother in his class and given a security detail of overindulgent older girls. This was the first time I was lost and found that girls are full of 'sugar and spice, and all things nice'.

I followed my brother from the Fort Convent kindergarten to Campion School, which was then a Jesuit primary school just around the corner. It was a 'double' promotion for me. I skipped the second standard, since my Mum wanted both her sons to be in the same school. It simplified the logistics of dropping us off and picking us up from the same place. But there I became a dropout. The teachers seemed uninterested in me so why would I be interested in them. I remember being ranked twenty-eighth out of thirty-two in third standard, thereby setting off a holy row at home. 'No one in the family has done so poorly,' I was scolded. Kit was always in the first four. But at least I'm not last, I thought. No one seemed to appreciate that.

By the fifth standard, I had fallen so far behind that Mum felt it would be best for me to repeat the class. Only then I realized this was serious business and I managed to get to the sixth standard, in St Mary's High School, Mazagaon, in 1952 with my brother, who was two years ahead of me now in the eighth standard. There the teachers brought me back into the mainstream and things began to change.

THE MICROCOSM

Originally founded as an Anglo-Indian orphanage in 1864, St Mary's was a cosmopolitan place where diverse classes and castes, religions and regions, ethnicities and races were represented. There were paupers and princes, Catholics and Protestants, Syrian Christians and Latins, Jews and gentiles, Malabaris and Goans, East Indians and Anglo-Indians from all the regions of the subcontinent and beyond. Indeed after the cotton boom during the American Civil War in the 1860s, Bombay was one of the most cosmopolitan cities in the world as the variety of head dresses seen at the Cotton Exchange demonstrated.

If Bombay was a microcosm of post-Partition India, St Mary's was a microcosm of the city. We were taught to value diversity as enriching, not diminishing. Here we made lifelong friends, forged loyalties that reached across seas and continents. We were three musketeers that hung together through thick and thin: Moses Taghioff, a Baghdadi Jew; Munawar Baig, a Konkani Muslim; and I, a Goan Christian.

The Jesuits I encountered there were my role models. They made the greatest impact on me not just when they taught in class but more so when they mixed with us on the playgrounds. This is where my journeying with the Jesuits began and now it has come full circle as I write these lines at Arrupe Niwas, lodged on the premises of the St Mary's campus. It is residence for those among us who need assisted care.

CREATIVE PEDAGOGY

Those early days at St Mary's privileged the sporting spirit and the 'scientific temper'. As students, we were encouraged to play team games on the field and to experiment in the labs with what we had learnt in class. We had many good and creative teachers. For instance, in the eight standard, Mr Giles Rebello taught us Indian history, not by having us memorize names, places and dates, but by encouraging us to speculate on why things happened as they did; not asking what Emperor Akbar or Chhatrapati Shivaji Maharaj did, but why they did it. We argued at length in class and in the bargain internalized the facts without having to 'mug them up' and got a better sense of history as well.

THE TROUBLEMAKER

Steam engines fascinated me with their huffing and puffing, such sound and fury from a little gaseous water, moving this huge mass of steel. So I tried it out on a quiet Sunday afternoon at home. I jammed a lid on an old beer can, filled it with water and set it on the stove. The explosion was deafening. In a trice I was out of the kitchen window and on to the terrace until things quietened down. No real damage was done, except perhaps to hypertensive hearts.

No wonder my mother would mourn: 'This Rudi, we don't know what he'll do next.'

To which family legend has recorded that I responded: 'But Mum, neither do I.'

'Rudi only has to look at my cut glass curios and they break,' she would exclaim in exasperation. But it wasn't my gaze that did the breaking, it was my little cycle that I raced around our large flat that scratched the polished furniture and toppled the curios. I began to feel like Dennis the Menace, who wondered why he got blamed for everything he did.

On one memorable occasion we were on a family outing. There was a squabble in the back seat of the car, where we children were piled in. This time Dad was really annoyed. He stopped the vehicle and ordered me out assuming I was the cause of the trouble.

'But Dad I didn't do anything,' I pleaded.

'Rudi! Get out,' he ordered again. I did and banged the door loudly after me. I went and sulked at the little garden at Ballard Bunder nearby which serviced the harbour launches; and with all the weight of nine years, I thought seriously: 'It's time for me to leave home.' But I had no idea of where to go or how to get there. So after a long struggle with myself, I limped back home, hungry, defeated and wounded, only to find the rest hadn't returned yet. What a wasted protest! Nobody seemed to have noticed it. Sometimes discretion is the better part of valour.

I was determined that my next protest—when I felt self-righteously wronged—would make its mark. So when the car was taken to the petrol pump to be refuelled I sneakily locked the car keys inside and disappeared. There was chaos and our poor chauffer had to take the blame and get the vehicle towed out of the way. He came home huffing and puffing and pointed me out to Dad as the culprit. This time as punishment I was given the cold shoulder by everybody at home—something I really hated. But it taught me not to indulge in such silly, spiteful reactions again.

LEARNING SELF-RELIANCE

My dad treated Kit and me as young adults even before we were teenagers. So when it came to renewing our radio license, he called the two of us and asked: 'Who listens to the radio the most?' We admitted that we did. And as a form of tax for its use, he told us, 'So now go and get the license. If you were paid employees, I might have told you where and how, but I want you to be independent, so go and find out.'

We had at no clue where to start. Mum was on our side or perhaps she didn't want us to be too independent too soon. She intervened with, 'But Jimmy, give them at least a little hint.'

'Go to the GPO,' was all he said.

The General Post Office was a ten-minute walk away. So there we were, two boys of ten and twelve, gazing up at this immense dome. Inside, there seemed to be hundreds of windows for transacting business, all spread over three storeys. Clearly we were lost, until a kindly gentleman pointed out the right place. We quickly paid the fee and came running home, triumphantly waving the license like a trophy. I felt like a grown-up—I could even get a radio license.

However, I still had to learn to hold my ground against the 'bigger badder' ever hungry boarders in school, who would insist on sharing my packed lunch from home. I did the wise thing. I just brought more lunch. The milk bottle that Mum insisted we take with our sandwiches would also be snatched away by a bigger boy: 'What? Drinking milk at your age? You should be ashamed!' And the bully would guzzle it down himself. So I stopped bringing any milk to school.

However, I enjoyed my years at St Mary's, as I believe, most of us did. The school prided itself on making 'young men' out of boys. We left school feeling 'rough and tough' and ready for the big bad world beyond the gates. In fact it might not really have been so. From St Mary's my group of school friends and I went on to St Xavier's College, another renowned Jesuit institution, which formed a protective cocoon in which we lived our undergrad life. And of course there were the girls from other English-medium schools who became part of the group. Our swagger might well have been something of a protective carapace.

St Xavier's opened for me new possibilities in the professional world at the time, primarily medicine and engineering that were considered to be promising careers for young men.

I felt intensely privileged to live at the centre of many intersections. A new post-colonial world was being put together, a new independent India was coming to birth, and my city by the sea was at the centre of it all.

BOMBAY TO MUMBAI

Many years later when I was in *vanvas*—exiled to the concrete jungle in Delhi—I wrote an elegy for the Bombay I grew up in, and what living there meant:

Mumbai Meri Jaan, Meri Rozi Roti, Meri Jivan Dharti

Where is the Bombay I knew and loved and felt so safe in? Where as children we would play in the streets and ride public transport without adult accompaniment, jumping in and out of running buses, trams and trains? The trams were the easiest and the best fun, they were so slow and safe. Roller skating behind ambling victorias trailing on a long rope was more risky. There was a time when everyone was welcome in the city by the sea, from north, south, east, west and yes, even from overseas. All could boast: Bumbai Meri Jaan, Meri Rozi Roti, Meri Jivan Dharti! But when Bombay became Mumbai, Mumbaikars became islanders, as when it was a fishing village, and the city seems no longer the gateway to an India of the future, but just an island off the west coast of Mahatashtra for 'sons of the soil'.

Without even noticing it, that time of innocence and abandon, of adventure and discovery seems lost forever. I wonder where the children play in this imploding city. If they do it must be in video parlours and probably war games to boot. Today Mumbai has become an unending struggle for life and livelihood. We are all becoming urban guerrillas in our own private wars, and perhaps mercenaries in some public ones, constantly redefining the outsider as the enemy: South Indian, North Indian, Muslim, Sikh... How has Bombay once the most cosmopolitan, the most populous, the wealthiest city in the country, become Mumbai for ethnocentric Mumbaikars only? Is this the future of urban India? A future that is already crashing into the present and so hauntingly described in Salvatore Quasimodo's epigraph:

> Each alone on the heart of the earth impaled
> upon a ray of sun:
> and suddenly it's evening.

Sudden tragedy makes us companions in pain, exploding into a city that never sleeps. As when there is a surprise terror attack. We stop for a while, pick up the pieces and then hurry on with what's left of our lives. But there's no guarantee that there isn't more of the same coming. Tragedy and pause punctuate our hurried, harried, hustled living! Yet soon enough we exorcise painful residues of haunting traumas. They make us resilient, but then perhaps too selective in our memories, for they have yet to teach us to share and care beyond the passing present. Life must go on and so it does. But how can our shared vulnerability make us more caring? When vengeance is compelling, how can forgiveness be our sword? Can we be instruments of peace together for each other, for all? How can the compassion that melds us together when some disaster strikes, work for lasting peace?

Mumbai has been bombed in 1993, 1997, 1998,

2002, 2003, 2004, and now 2006. Every monsoon brings disrupting flooding. In July 2005 a cloud burst brought most a metre of rain in three hours, which paralysed the city for over a week. The citizens pitched in to save the day. What next? There should be a system of 'quotas' for these disruptions! And in the meantime, we just have to hang in there and hope that if not good sense, at least common sense will prevail. Too many of those who want to teach others a lesson seemed to have learned the wrong ones themselves. For without a collective consensus, which still evades us, we can only end up more divided and more helpless, each alone and impaled by fear.

But we don't seem to be able to get our act together, to get a handle on where we are and why we keep going. But we are moving, moving on a carousel, round and round, up and down, while some people from the outside, we'd like to think, take potshots at us. Sometimes it's the rain gods who send us tsunamis from the sky; sometimes it's the demons on the ground who use terror against the defenceless. Yes, we are ever so proud of our city, Mumbai meri jaan! But how do we heal and cope with our brokenness? Surely, we need more than just the spontaneous generosity that a disaster evokes. This calls for a more sustained human fellowship of mutual respect and personal freedom, and we still have a long way to get there.

Travelling on the suburban trains in the city, I remember reading a railway notice: 'Young and old persons are travelling unaccompanied; please accommodate them and look after them.' Today the notice would read: Do not befriend strangers, report any suspicious persons. I tell myself if there's a blast in the crowded train, I may just see the flash, I might not even hear the noise. And then, if I'm lucky, for me there'll be just silence, and hopefully light, not darkness! Maybe that will be the only light at the end of this tunnel. But what of the others left behind in the dark? What kind of city will be left for them? They still must board the trains for a livelihood. Mumbai, meri rozi roti!

The next time I'm on the train, I'll close my eyes and when I open them again, hope the city will still be there, and those unimaginable horrors prove just imaginary? It's a game I used to play as a child when I was frightened and alone. I seem to be going back to my roots. But I can't run away from my life, my livelihood, my home? And if I do leave Mumbai, will Mumbai ever leave me? Mumbai meri jaan, Mumbai meri rozi roti, Mumbai meri jivan dharti!

(July 2006)

THE SEARCHER

I do remember feeling that my life must be lived for something bigger than a successful career for myself and I was looking for role models. My dad was the secretary of the Goan Liberation Council in the 1950s and worked with Ronald D'Sousa, a full-time party cadre of the Communist Party of India (CPI), assigned by the party to facilitate the Goa liberation movement. D'Sousa claimed his devoted mother's prayers for his conversion back to the Catholic Church only made him a better Communist. My dad, though a businessman himself, was all admiration for him, and his commitment and dedication to his party. He lived in the party chummery on dal and rice with five rupees as a monthly allowance. He might well have been my role model and I might have joined his party if I had taken to politics.

I was a young man in search of a cause to dedicate myself to, something to work for, to be committed to, something personally fulfilling and challenging. In the institutions that educated me, the Jesuits represented a model of dedication and commitment that attracted and challenged me profoundly. Why can't I be like that? I would wonder.

But I was still hesitant to take the plunge. There was so much else in life I wanted to experience. Would I have the staying power to see this venture through to the end? That was my deepest and most consistent doubt. As I wrestled with these doubts, I gradually began to realize intuitively that if I did really want to make a difference for others in this world and be happy and feel fulfilled doing it, I could never do that by living selfishly for myself. I had to live for others, not just my family and friends. That would be a very small world. I wanted a larger world. But that world would only be as large as my heart. So then how large was my heart? And how deep did I want my dedication to this world to be?

I realized, too, I was gratuitously privileged in so many aspects of my life. I had never known hunger or want as so many of my lesser privileged fellow Indians had. There had been no question about my being educated, nor was there any question that my sisters should be either. I had been allowed to choose what I wanted to study. If I were to look around me, I would be saying, 'There but for the grace of God go I', a hundred, a thousand times a day.

But just saying it would not change things. If much had been given to me, much would be expected from me too. Somewhere, I felt I had to help make a difference to those less privileged than I. But I didn't want to do that premised on negative feelings such as anger or guilt. I knew intuitively again that those would ruin my life and worse, they would poison the lives of those I was trying to help. Moreover, I was taught at home and school that mere sentimental sympathy or the passive pity of 'do-gooders' only did more harm than good in the long run. It just made one feel good about oneself without making any real difference.

THE JESUS MYTH

Finally, it was the 'Jesus myth' I was internalizing on my spiritual pilgrimage that began to trump all else in my own life: to walk this earth as He did, bring healing and wholeness to broken and betrayed lives, to live the beatitudes He taught, bring to birth a brave new world, to pour out my life in libation on the desert sand in the hope it would bloom into as oasis of joy and hope. Eventually, I believed it would grow into a garden of Eden, where every tear would be wiped away from every eye, and death would be no more, leaving only moksha and nirvana for all. This Jesus was internalized, so gradually that it was difficult to articulate and share along the way then—as it is even now.

This is not just the historical Jesus we read about in the Gospels, not only the Christ of faith we learn about in Christian tradition. It is the Jesus whose 'mimesis' (imitation) transforms my own life and becomes the deepest longing of my being, this unconditional, inclusive love of my Ishtadevata, who excludes nothing good and beautiful, brave and strong, gentle and caring…wherever it's found.

Moreover, wherever such good is renounced for the greater good, the common good, it is never lost but comes back a hundredfold. The Sufis sung of such a one: Allah hoo, Alla hoo. The Sant-kavis taught this: Ram the satvik, the saumya, the maryada, the utkarsh Purush, found in all religious traditions. The Bohidsattvas practise and preach this. St Mother Teresa of Calcutta summed it up: I love all religions, but I'm in love with my own.

TAKING THE PLUNGE

In my second year of college—this was in 1959—a missionary gave us our annual retreat, and I decided to burn my boats and take the plunge. The retreat Director took me to see the novice-master, Fr Aloysius Coyne, in Vinayalaya, Andheri, then a forested suburb of Bombay city. I told him I would apply to enter the novitiate the next year.

His response was sober: 'Well, my son,' he said calmly, 'June is many months away. We'll see when the time comes.'

It was late in the year, around October when we had this conversation. He must have thought the next six months or so would give me a cooling-off period, a time for reflection. He must have had his own doubts too. I was impulsive and had to learn the patience needed to make mature and discerning decisions. This one, he must have suspected, was on the spur of a retreat. This was a big decision perhaps the biggest of my life till then, and I hadn't so much as discussed it with my family or my friends in any serious manner.

Oftentimes I have been asked: why did you become a Jesuit. Or at times even more pointedly: 'How did *you* ever become one of *them*?' Sometimes the question is posed out of light-hearted curiosity; sometimes it is occasioned by earnest surprise; sometimes it is thrown at me with a little disappointment and even disgust. But even when the question comes from a genuine interest and concern, I find it extremely difficult to answer. I don't know where to begin—or how to end. It is a question which is so personal and all-embracing, that I am always a little afraid that something of the personal mystery will be lost in the answer or that my story may not make the same sense to the other—if indeed it makes sense at all. It's analogous to falling in love. You really aren't sure it has happened until it already has. As Blaise Pascal said long ago: 'The heart has its reasons of which reason knows nothing of.'

BEING THE BEST CLOWN

In my mind, however, I was quite clear that I wanted to become a Jesuit. I am not sure if the priesthood attracted me at that time but if I had to be a priest to become a Jesuit, then that was what I would do. Not that all my doubts had been miraculously swept away. But in conscience, I felt I had to give the Jesuit option a fair try, or I'd be running away from myself for the rest of my life. In all fairness, I felt I had to break the news first at home. I went to tell my father of my decision to join the Jesuits—I decided that I might as well beard the lion in his den.

So sometime in the summer of 1960, I went to see my dad in his office. His secretary showed me into his cabin and hovered around, waiting for instructions.

'Can I speak to you?' I asked my father.

'Go ahead,' he said, putting down the documents

he was holding with the resigned air of a man who had better things to do than would allow his young son to disrupt him at work, which I guess might have been important.

'Alone?' I added.

He looked mildly surprised and then realized I meant his secretary, so he asked her to leave.

With as little beating about the bush as possible, I told him I was going to join the Jesuits.

'Well, we can talk about it later, can't we?' he asked.

'Dad,' I said, 'you will be getting a letter from Fr Provincial accepting me into the Society of Jesus sometime this week.' (Actually, the letter arrived the next day!) He might have been annoyed at being disturbed at work but he was really upset at not having been consulted and that I was presenting him with what he saw as a fait accompli.

'Do you live in a home or is this just a hotel,' he asked, 'for you to come and go as you please? Surely we should have some say in this?'

When he realized this was something I had to decide and try out myself, if only to be certain whether or not this was the right place for me, he finally said: 'Well then, become a clown if you must; only be the best Jesuit clown in the world.'

To my mother, he said: 'The boy's a joker; he can't be serious, he's just clowning.'

In the weeks before I left for the novitiate, the first phase in the 'making of a Jesuit', an initiation which lasts two years, my mother would often call me to sit by her bed after supper, and I, a restless nineteen-year-old, would grumble, 'Now what?' and she'd let me go. Till one day she simply heaved a tearful sigh, 'I just want look at you, my son!' she said.

Just nineteen, still trembling on the brink of new worlds opening up before me, I couldn't grasp the depth of a mother's love for her son—made all the more precious because of the nuisance he had been—who was now abruptly leaving her.

It took me many years to realize what that must have meant to both my parents; and how they were trusting me to an open-ended future, which they could only follow with their prayers. Yes, I had a whole new future opening before me; they had a past that was closing in on them. And I began to realize how they were the ones actually making the bigger sacrifice, and how I must never betray their trust and love.

Some days after I broke the news of my joining the Jesuits, my Mum went to see to the Novice Master and complained, 'Fr Coyne, I have only two sons and you are taking one away.'

With Jesuitical insight, he replied, 'Mrs Heredia, it has been my experience that many mothers in your position later find that they have only one son, the one who becomes a Jesuit.' My mother realized how true this was as with time her four other children married and moved on with families of their own, especially when she was left widowed in 1975 till she passed away in 2013.

NEW ADVENTURE

I think about the name my mother had for the family: 'the dear octopus' she called it. She had insisted that she was a D'Silva before becoming a Heredia. And now one of the arms of the octopus was detaching itself. The family at large, I believe, saw it as a disruption. For me it was a new adventure and the beginning of a new way of life; for those left behind at home, it was disloyalty to the clan.

I was asked: 'But why the Jesuits?' Others in the family warned: 'You'll never get to be a bishop or a cardinal.' In fact I was sent to meet a prince of the church, Valerian Cardinal Gracias, at Archbishop's House, Bombay, before I finally entered the novitiate. He did not try to interfere with my choices; he only asked me to consider the diocesan alternative.

The diocesan priests are the bureaucracy of the Catholic Church. They administer the parishes in the diocese and are responsible to their bishop for running them and the other institutions of the local church therein assigned to them, such as the parish schools. Like all Catholic priests, they are bound by clerical celibacy.

Religious men and women take vows of poverty, i.e., to share their goods in common and live a simple life in community; and of obedience, i.e., to their appointed superiors as regards their allotted assignments and work; and finally, of chastity i.e., to live chaste, celibate lives. They are similar to monks and nuns that most religious traditions have. Though there are differences in how the religious live out their vows: some disengage from the world into a life of prayer and meditation, and others are actively involved with it, striving to make a difference for the better. And some live lives that integrate both contemplation and action. This is what made the Jesuit way of life so attractive to me: men committed to solid virtue and solid learning, in the world but not of it.

The Jesuit vocation promoter I knew in school earlier—whom we called the 'big fisherman', for his close reading of Matthew 4:19, 'Behold I will make you fishers of men'—turned me off. He was forever 'fishing', casting wide his net on all sides on his boat, to harvest the waters for unsuspecting fish. Rather it was the patient Jesuit priest, Father Jaime Fabregat, who turned me into a wannabe Jesuit simply by listening to me when I poured out my miseries and my doubts. He won me over to the Jesuits precisely by *not* trying; while the travelling salesman, who was over-selling his goods and seemed bent on hustling me into the Society, was turning me off.

When told the Jesuits take the vow of poverty but diocesan priests practise it, I really had no answer, because it cut so close to the bone. The big monies then were in social projects and foreign funding found its way to the Jesuits, not the pastoral ministries. The local contributions of the many poor parishes of the archdiocese were barely enough to sustain them, let alone to provide for the old, sick and retired priests of the diocese. Finally my mother put paid to this 'poverty' trope with her firm: 'Better the devil we know, than the devil we don't.'

Today both protagonists, diocesan priests and religious men, look rather similar. And now I think, if I had known more diocesan priests, they might well have been my role models too.

CELIBACY

I had four cousins who had already joined the Society, so when it became known that I was joining too, my family felt that this was going too far. Surely four young men were enough of an offering to the Church? After all, we could all be going out and having children, furthering the family bloodlines. And then there was always the question they weren't going to ask you: 'You're going to take a vow of celibacy. How will you manage?'

This must have been the reason why my college gang thought this was some kind of joke. They just didn't believe I'd go through with it. For a nineteen-year-old, a vow of celibacy is a big issue. It would be difficult. But I believed it would get easier with time. Biology was on my side on that one. So if it was such a large part of my renunciation, I thought, I might as well throw in poverty and obedience as add-ons.

Fr Jaime Fabregat was wise. He cautioned me,

'Celibacy may or may not get easier, but obedience gets harder as we grow older and wiser than our superiors.' And there indeed was the rub as I found out soon enough. Though I'm not sure if it was because I was getting wiser with age, or my superiors sillier with time. However, clowns know how to cope with the ridiculous in others as in oneself, spread good humour and bring good cheer.

CHECKING THEM OUT

For a little while I enjoyed being the centre of attention. Filled with self-importance, I decided to check these Jesuits out myself. Not yet a pre-novice, I went to see the provincial superior, Fr Aixala, residing in St Xavier's High School, the priest in charge of the Bombay Province. I asked him what the Jesuits did with all their money. He was a kindly old man so he listened to me and must have been puzzled by my query but his answer was a wall.

'That's our business,' he replied shortly, 'Others don't need to know.'

I almost lost my vocation on the spot. I vividly remember walking round the corner from the school to the college and wondering how I could trust these Jesuits when they were so secretive about their monies; what had they to hide? What sort of secret 'business' was this? As I stood in the quadrangle of the college, memorialized in so many films, some young men were playing basketball. I thought of the Jesuits from my childhood. I thought of the college itself. I thought of all the good the Society of Jesus was doing here and in so many places elsewhere. And I thought: 'I can't be guided by my dark suspicions; I can use them as a searchlight. I do not need to put the Society on the witness stand of my prosecution, at least not yet.'

Later I realized this answer was a gentle rebuke from Fr Provincial. Perhaps it was intended in zen-koan fashion to have the very effect it would have. The wall was not something I could climb. It was not even something I could bang my head against. But if I could acknowledge the existence of the wall, if I could find a way to have faith despite its existence, why then I might understand the vow of obedience I would one day have to take to become a Jesuit.

LEAVING HOME

The day I left home, my friends trooped in to say goodbye. I took a final look around the house before the immediate family piled into the car and we drove the fifteen-odd miles to the novitiate, almost in silence punctured now and then with feigned cheer. To break the darkening mood, I said: 'Please don't treat me like a dead man walking; at least not yet. I have no intention of suicide either.'

The master of novices greeted all of us warmly and we said our stoic goodbyes with pretended cheerfulness.

Only as they drove away down the hill did I get a glimpse through the rear window of the car of my mum wiping her tears with edge of her sari.

Later, this is how she recalled the moment:

The Parting

'But Mother (he always called me Mother, in moments of stress) it's true, that's what I have decided.'

I look at him in pain. Can this be my little boy? Not so very long ago... But I am talking as if it was so long ago, when in reality, it was only yesterday that I handled him on my knee and held him up for his father to tweak a button nose.

Aloof and Remote

Today he seems remote and very aloof, wise with the weight of his nineteen years. He talks to me like the United Nations charter, of the right to choose, the right to live one's own life, and the crying need in the world for the kind of men he wishes to join. He talks endlessly in the didactic drone of an adult striving to drive home a point. Occasionally, I interrupt that he is young, idealistic, therefore impractical. But to this he recommends hotly that I read a certain essay entitled 'Wanted—One Impractical Man'. To save the world of course! There is nothing then that I can say to further my plaint. The case is lost, the situation beyond recall.

Details

So we get down to the inescapable details, a kit that has to be got in accordance with the list, farewell visits, and mundane affairs that have to be settled. To me there is a tragic finality about it all, which seems to escape him completely. He chirrups around the house like a starling at dawn. I look through all his belongings with a leaden heart. 'This is surely how a death in the house must feel,' I think to myself and I urge him to take everything, his silly knickknacks, brightly-coloured shirts, the paraphernalia of rusty scrap, which had given him so many an hour of pure untainted pleasure, and conversely almost succeeded in changing me into a fault-finding shrew for the rest of my life.

But he has no use for these things of the past. The past! Ah, that is the relevant word. To me and to the others at home it is. To him there is a shining future, beckoning gloriously from the top of the hill.

It's a beautifully sunny afternoon the day he has to leave, contrary to all the predictions of the clerk of the weather. Everything has been done for the last time, his last dinner, his last tea, his last long look around the house. That is how we see it and we tell him so, but his reaction as usual is beautifully normal. 'I don't know why everybody insists on treating me like a man condemned. I have no intention at all of committing suicide, I assure you!' We all laugh heartily at this typical quip and a breath of sunshine seems to lift some of the gloom.

Memories

And then his friends come pouring in to send him off in true tribal style, with war-cries and mock chants and snake-dancing demonstrations. Thanks to them it's beautifully normal again as we chug

> up the little slope into the porch of the Novitiate. There are so many 'parents' around and so many smiling young novices that there is really no time at all for the waterworks to burst. We see him as we leave, a slight figure in civvies, waving bravely at our receding vehicle. How easy it's been after all. 'Tis only when we return home that the echoes and memories spring at us from every corner. This dear house truly comes 'to eat us up', as they say in our beautiful mother tongue of a place which is devoid of a loved one's presence.
>
> But not for long. This he has promised. Already through the tears we can distinguish the blurred lines of the priestly shape, many long years hence, undoubtedly, but nevertheless it is there, the outline of a man of God.
>
> (Irene Heredia, 1960)

I should have realized much earlier that all through her pain at my parting, she had more faith in me than I had in myself.

MEANINGFUL NOVITIATE

I entered the novitiate with a certain curiosity. I had to do this, I had to find out what it was all about and if I really was meant to be a Jesuit or not. I found the novitiate really quite hard and tense: my fellow novices were not known to me; the time schedule was very tight and broken into bits and pieces leaving little time to oneself. There were all kinds of small demands that were often somewhat annoying and sometimes seemed even ridiculous. At times I was waiting to see whether I would be sent back. I could imagine myself walking out quite happily. Now I am glad I didn't.

One of my school friends, Dinshaw Burjorjee, visited me rather early in my Jesuit life at Vinayalaya. After I showed him around, he asked as we stood on the little hillock overlooking the city: 'Rudi, tell me really if you're happy here.' And I paused and quite sincerely and spontaneously responded: 'I don't know, but I do know that I have found meaning here.' For happiness was not the deciding factor in my joining the Jesuits, but rather it was my own search for something more meaningful in my life, something to live by. I saw, in the many Jesuits I knew, role models for me. And I felt compelled to give such a life a fair try. That's precisely what the novitiate was meant for.

I felt even more inspired as I realized Jesuit spirituality is quintessentially other-, rather than self-oriented. I have experienced that what I've renounced has become a blessing a hundred times over and above; what I've given away has returned to me a hundredfold and more, pressed down and overflowing. Looking back, I can say, here I have found acceptance and companionship, and much love as well, both within the Society and beyond.

So now, I write:

Looking Back

Despite all these turns and twists
and ups and downs,

my cup brims over in gratitude.
Though I've often wondered
about what might have been,
I don't regret the path I've trod.
Looking back from where I'm at
The wonderful things that happened
already now but not fully yet.

LIGHT AND DARKNESS

When I began my religious life on 20th June 1960, we were in the pre-Vatican II years, when 'canonical cloister' separated residential areas for men and women as a requirement for religious communities. One kept in touch with one's family through a monthly letter home. One visited one's own home just thrice a year for a family meal, even if one was posted in the same town: Christmas, Easter, one's birthday and perhaps for the funeral of an immediate family member. You needed special permission to stay overnight at home. Little wonder for my mother, as she would tell me later, it was like 'a death in the family'.

However, I was fortunate to meet Jesuits who made the life and commitment the Society demanded more reasonable without compromising the challenge it offered. I remember an incident during the first probation, the week or so before the novitiate formally began, when the would-be novices got a closer look at the Society and vice versa. I was standing in the corridor reading a brochure on the 'rules of modesty' novices were expected to follow and I was getting more and more alarmed and depressed because they seemed to have been designed to construct a prison for the self. There were rules about everything—about how to hold one's head, how to place one's hands, how to walk, how to sit...

I was thinking to myself: 'This is a strait-jacket!'

Fr Henry Pascual, one the senior Jesuits, was passing by in the corridor when he noticed that I was looking rather grim.

'What's getting you down?' he asked.

I showed him the booklet. 'Look at this. This is a prison!' I said to him.

He looked at brochure and then said rather dismissively, 'Oh, the *Rules of Modesty*! Listen, nothing here is difficult. If you find anything difficult, it means that you have misunderstood it by taking it out of context.'

The context of these rules was mediaeval; they had been devised when St Ignatius imagined the Jesuit as a 'very parfait gentil' religious Christian. In other words, right from his candidacy, a would-be Jesuit was to be a satvik person who eschewed the tamasik and the rajasik. But what I had missed was that this was an ideal to be pursued, not a goal already attained. That lifted a burden off my soul. I was too literal a novice. I still had to learn how to set a text in its context, without compromising it. 'Nothing difficult, just misunderstood,' became my shibboleth for the rest of my novitiate! I was still to realize that the Society calls us to maturity and daring, even as we stretch ourselves to measure up to make a meaningful offering, *obsequium rationale*. I still had to realize the paradox: if you love something, it's always easy; as we love, so we live; what we love changes us; whom we love transforms us!

THE POST-CONCILIAR CHURCH

The novitiate then was really quite standardized, very much the same all over the Society. This was before Vatican II and before the Society of Jesus had made its adaptation to the post-Vatican II Church. At the time of my joining the Jesuits, the Catholic Church was on the threshold of big changes with premonitions of a new Ecumenical (Universal) Council to be called. What would this mean for the post-War Church? The two World Wars had already changed the map of the post-colonial world. Could there be a change coming in the post-Conciliar Church? There was excitement in the air.

There have been many upheavals in the church in the centuries before the Protestant Reformation of the 16th century which divided Christendom. The Council of Trent (1545–63) was the defensive Catholic response of the Roman Church to Protestantism that locked it into a 'fortress Catholicism' for four centuries. This was a long time of stasis, some might even say stagnation. Even if that is a harsh judgement on this period, undeniably the Church was out of sync with the modern world. The Second Vatican Council, (1963–66) called by Pope John XXIII, was meant to update (aggiornamento, he called it) the Roman Catholic Church. Good Pope John opened a window to let in some fresh air and there came a whirlwind that eventually blew many off their feet and brought down the old walls of the 'fortress'. Many of the Conciliar reforms were resisted vigorously by some conservative council members, but once accepted by the assembly there was no turning back. The new liturgy was just the most obvious change of many more radical ones.

MELDING INTO THE MOULD

The Novice Master, Fr Aloysius Coyne, was a gentle grandfather to us all. He was in his sixties and I was just nineteen when I joined. He had exquisite manners, was always soft-spoken and yet never a push-over. He seemed to be everything St Ignatius wanted a Jesuit to be. His interest in, and concern for, me I found very reassuring. It personalized his accompaniment through my years in the novitiate. I think he changed my orientation to spirituality in a very fundamental way when he gave me some spiritual theology to read.

I had raced through the required spiritual reading which I thought urgently needed an update. For instance, one of the texts was *The Practice of Christian and Religious Perfection* by Fr Alphonsus Rodriguez, in three volumes, which dated back to 1609! But then I remember finding in the novitiate library, Fr Hugo Rahner's *The Spirituality of St. Ignatius Loyola: An Account of Its Historical Development*. It was in those pages that I learnt that Jesuit spirituality is a mysticism in action, an identification with Jesus. Here I encountered the Jesus of faith who carried the Jesuit mission to the world. Fr Coyne gave me Hugo Rahner's *Selected Letters of St Ignatius to Women*. I wondered why, and he told me to see how affectionate Ignatius was in his letters and yet how spiritual he was at the same time. I think that gave me an insight, for which I am ever grateful. It debunked for me the machismo to which we Jesuits are so prone.

For me there was another very significant person in the novitiate, Fr Frederick Sopena, the Socius (assistant) to the Novice Master, and I must say I am extremely grateful to him too. One day he must have seen me looking very tense, I suppose, or maybe just depressed. He called me to his room and said sit down here, and he looked me in the eye and said: 'Rudi, if you are going to become a saint, you are going to become St Rudi Heredia, not St Aloysius Coyne. Do you understand? Now get out and get on with the rest of your life.'

That was such a relief, another burden was lifted, a burden I did not even know I had been carrying. I found a new freedom! I realized in a flash that a nineteen-year-old novice like me might find a spiritual inspiration in Fr Coyne, the saintly sixty-five-year-old Novice Master, but he couldn't be a behavioural role model for me. I had first to be myself and then allow grace to build on nature, to be my own 'man', before I could be a 'man of God', or I'd end up as a charlatan mimic living off cheap grace.

Once you get used to the routine of the novitiate, it simply carries you along. So I told myself: you just have to get up in the morning and recite the *Te Deum*, a hymn of praise and thanksgiving to God. It was usually recited in Latin at the top of one's voice to help wake up! Then the rest of the day would follow and it would be time to go to sleep!

A NEW WORLD

My novitiate at Vinayalaya was a time of innocence and enthusiasm, a new world was opening and we were all rearing to go. I look back to it with nostalgia for it was my Bethlehem, the house of bread, the place where I was born as a Jesuit. When I need to recall my personal journey as a Jesuit, I visit there in imagination, making a 'composition of place', as Ignatius taught in his book of the Spiritual Exercises. And my visits there are still a mini pilgrimage to the nostalgia of long ago and far away, where I learnt that a true Jesuit is one who is not intimidated by the greatest and yet stands by the least; this is truly Godly ('*Non cohiberi a maximo, contineri tamen a minimo, hoc divinum est*').

Thanks to this and other teachings and life experiences, I mellowed much along the way as

I journeyed with my fellow Jesuits who became companions and friends. I gained from lived values and role models of the many Jesuits who were doing valuable work quietly, labouring in His vineyards in any number of unlikely settings. I have learned from conversations with women at village 'wells of living waters' and with brothers on the road to Emmaus, recognizing this death-life mystery in the breaking and sharing of bread. There were the communities of lived dialogue which challenged me to change the false gods of worldly success and financial prosperity for the true gold of the spirit, of freedom and joy. And dared to take risks when one is involved with the least and the last, because as the Master taught us and I have come to believe: 'It is more blessed to give than receive' (Acts 20:35).

There was the constant requirement to respect difference (the many-sidedness of truth, the anekantavad) and actively make peace through dialogue to become children of God in one family, vasudaiva kutumbakam (the world is one family). I learned to curb self-righteous anger, which makes us hypocritical and rajasik; to actively seek peace for one's inner self and make peace with others, to become satvik, for peacemakers are the blest children of God. I came to experience that to forgive is the condition for being forgiven. I had to learn the hard way that a suffering love can be redemptive as well, and that ultimately, 'Joy is the only infallible sign of God's presence' as Teilhard de Chardin said, and our rishis and roshis, our Sufis and sants all taught. The ultimate reality I learnt was sat-chit-anandam (the trinity of being-consciousness-bliss).

CHALLENGING FAITH

I learned a challenging faith from the doubting Thomases I encountered along the way. I learned to listen respectfully to the doubt while believing in the doubter. I found they were often of greater comfort to me when I encountered my dark nights of the soul, more so than those who would offer the pablum of easy comfort. I found reassurance in the good Samaritans I met along the way, and I struggled to find forgiveness in my heart for the bad ones because I knew that I might often find myself numbered among them. I walked with the sadness and shame I felt when I fell on my path, and experienced joy and gratitude when I was picked up by soulmates I had bonded with, and companions I had prayed with…

But none of it was easy. Nor do I think I would have wanted it to be. One learns to mistrust that which comes easily. Like in Hilaire Belloc's 'Prophet Lost in the Hills at Evening':

> I challenged and I kept the Faith,
> The bleeding path alone I trod;
> It darkens. Stands about my wraith,
> And harbour me—Almighty God!

The novitiate lasts two years. Most of my first year in the novitiate I spent subconsciously hoping I'd be sent home. I even asked Father Coyne, the Novice Master, how could I be trusted to live the ideals being proposed to novices like me. I hit the bottom of the pit when he said he had advised Fr Provincial to make me wait two years and complete my college graduation before being accepted into the novitiate but the Provincial overruled him. Jesuits have a fine-tuned system of checks and balances: Provincials have the final word on who is admitted; Novice Masters on who stays. So now I stayed, disabused of any sense of superiority over my fellow Novices.

Little by little I was bonded with my fellow Jesuits into a group of 'friends in the Lord' and 'companions on mission'. This was less a commitment to institutional structures and regulations than a shared way of life, 'our way of proceeding'. And as for role models, I found in Father Sopena's briskness and camaraderie combined with a deep spiritual life a more appropriate role model than in the saintliness of Father Coyne. Freddy Sopena was someone I could realiztically emulate, even as a clown.

The second year of the Jesuit novitiate ended with our first vows of perpetual poverty, chastity and obedience. We were now Jesuit scholastics, as Jesuit seminarians in training are called. Not that we were scholars already, but as Jesuits we are called to be both men of solid virtue and solid learning, the novitiate was meant to be an initiation into Jesuit spirituality. Now began a rigorous training in laying the foundation for further learning. Both dimensions were to be integrated into an apostolic mission which reached out to others.

REMEDIAL LEARNING

The year of the juniorate followed, 1962–63, devoted to the humanities, and a brief introduction to classical literature which opened a whole new world of 'rhetoric' for us. This was a challenge I felt I could meet and which I felt good about too. It was a kind of remedial year for the classroom education I had received in school and college, opening new worlds to explore. Here I learnt how to write and found others with similar interests as well. I certainly felt reassured at being accepted by my teachers, who were role models for us young Jesuit scholastics. We were all on the same trip as friends in the Lord and companions on mission.

As an apostolic outreach programme, we juniors were assigned to teach catechism in the nearby parishes. I was assigned to teach the seventh-standard schoolchildren in Our Lady of Egypt in Kalina. In anticipation of Vatican II's liturgical reform, the Church had begun cleaning up its altars. St Philomena, once a very popular saint and martyr, had just been 'decanonized'. She was no longer a saint because new historical scholarship pointed to her being a mythical figure. But the conservative parish priest would have none of this 'demythologization'. He argued, 'If she were a myth, how could she have been a saint for centuries? How can you come along one fine day and say she's to be taken off the altar?'

This was the line taken by a girl in the last row of the class. With her parish priest on her side, she kept insisting that St Philomena was 'a virgin and martyr'.

Finally, someone pulled me aside and told me what this was all about. 'Brother, her name is Philomena.'

That explained her cussedness.

LANGUAGE SCHOOL

Although I was born and bred in Bombay, I didn't know a word of Marathi, so four of us juniors, as we were called, were sent for a year to the language school in Nashik, located on 'Jail Road', on the way to the Central Government in the town. We were four young scholastics studying together, with an affable tutor and a seventy-four-year-old superior in rather indifferent health. If only old Fr Stanny Fernandes's health had been as good as his Marathi!

In Nashik, I was again teaching catechism to the seventh-standard children in the convent school next door. In my first week there, a girl in the front row kept raising her hand—fist closed and her little finger pointing up. I kept urging her to put her hand down and she kept lifting it up repeatedly. I thought she wanted to ask me something she was too shy to ask. After a bit of this back and forth, she just rushed out of classroom. The boys, grinning from ear to ear, were happy to explain she was indicating her urgent need to the bathroom, while the girls shyly giggled into their sleeves. I must have seemed a really ignorant clown to the whole class not to have understood the gesture. But sometimes even such miscommunication in good faith can make for positive relations, especially with primary school students. Later I was told she was already engaged and the fiancé might come after me! So I quickly made peace with her.

But there were also times when I could be impatient. I remember talking to the Provincial and saying, 'I don't think Father Stanny understands us young scholastics.'

He frowned. 'There are so many young people who look after their parents. Why can't you put up with this?'

I responded, 'I thought the superior was there to look after us!'

He shook his head: 'In a community, we look after each other.'

That was a reality check for me on Jesuit obedience and our relationship to the superior.

But there was comic relief in this small community too. As when once Fr Peter Lewis—the over-worked local parish priest—fell fast asleep during the longish homily, his assistant, Fr Banon, was preaching at the Sunday evening Mass. When Fr Banon finally wound down, Fr Peter was deep in the arms of Morpheus. Finally an altar boy had to be detailed to wake him up. He woke up with a start.

'What—who?' he said, sitting up, rubbing his eyes.

I don't know who was more embarrassed—he, the congregation, or Fr Banon!

Eventually, we learnt enough Marathi to celebrate the Lenten liturgy and thankfully we got through without the need for any alarm clocks.

QUINZAINE IN KHANDALA

Traditionally Jesuit scholastics had a two-week vacation each summer in a cooler clime. We called it 'quinzaine' following the French tradition. We had ours in our villas at the foothills of the Western Ghats in the hill station of Khandala. We went for long walks, enjoying the cool, clean air and the simple but hearty meals. This exercise of muscular Christianity was encouraged though the local superior did have a word of caution. 'Try not to take too many risks; falling off a mountain is not an approved way of dying in the Society of Jesus,' he said. But that hardly dampened our enthusiasm to explore the rugged terrain.

I still remember the points for our daily meditation once proposed by Fr George Soares, the spiritual father of the holiday camp, on the dangers, not *to* but *of* the vows, at least for us scholastics.

Poverty was enjoined upon us but instead of helping us share more generously and care more concernedly for the things we used, since we held all in common, it could make us more irresponsible because we were provided with everything we needed, and could be accountable for nothing we used.

In maintaining our vows of chastity, we might focus selfishly on our own virtue, not with being truly concerned and loving and caring, as evangelical celibacy, for the sake of the kingdom is meant to be.

The vow of obedience, rather than making us available and eager for mission, could sap our initiative and leave us childish, ever waiting for orders, never taking responsibility. The evangelical life was an invitation to live a life fully human, fully open to the divine or in other words: Be totally committed, completely detached.

Here in our scholastic years of training, we laid the foundation of our companionship in community life and our teamwork in a common corporate mission, and experienced 'how good and joyful it is to live as brothers united' (Psalm 133). I am bonded to the Society through my friends in the Lord, my companions in mission, not institutionalized rules and regulations. This is the divine love that St Ignatius places at the very beginning of the Constitution as its foundation, though he admits Constitutions make sense only if they help us to deal with the weakness of our human nature. In other words, the Constitution of the Jesuits was not meant to found an institution but to bond together a band of brothers.

LEARNING JESUIT OBEDIENCE

Once after our quinzaine, on our way back to Nashik from Khandala, I asked if I could break journey halfway at Kaylan, some 50 kms from Mumbai, and attend my elder brother's wedding two days later in Bombay. The same Provincial who thought it fitting that scholastics look after their elderly superiors as parents, replied saying, 'You'd do better praying for your brother in Nashik.' He was an alien who did not understand what a first wedding in an Indian family might mean to the parents. To internalize and accept this decision certainly wasn't easy and I know my brother still hasn't forgiven the Jesuits for it either. But then I didn't join the Jesuits because I thought they're all perfect, but to try to become more 'perfect' myself.

So I returned to Nashik to find myself alone in the house; the Superior had gone for a break, and the others scholastics had left too, one for an exam, another to see a doctor and the third to visit a dentist or someone else. Some provinces did have such Provincials, and their tribe still survives, though most are more moderate and dialogic after Vatican II.

Experiences like these helped me realize that obedience must be a dialogue to discern God's will for the greater common good, and even if the superior fails, the subject should not follow suit. For sometimes in this dialogue, one side or the other may need to be reminded that religious obedience binds, in conscience, the subject to obey in trust, just as much as it does the superior to command for the sake of mission; anything less is an abuse of the superior's authority and the goodwill of the subject. It compromises religious obedience profoundly. A Jesuit under obedience must then represent his side, as emphatically as it warrants. Though the superior has the last and final word, a Jesuit subject always has the second last word.

Once we heard of a Jesuit who had been ordered out of his Provincial's office. He shot back: 'You are my Provincial. I have a right to speak to you, I will not get out. You can get out if you want.' I was so shocked. This was a man who many of us had taken as a role model. I went to Fr Sopena and said: 'Here was a Jesuit who was such a role model—a truly charismatic man on a mission—and look what he said!' Once again Fr Sopena sat me down and reassured me: 'Brother, that is the power of true holiness. Don't you see that such men are afraid of nothing?'

And so I learnt that just as Jesuit authority must never be merely dictatorial or domineering, Jesuit obedience must never be passive or fearful. It must always be dialogical. Few are aware that every Jesuit has the right to appeal to the Superior General over the heads of all the intervening authorities, and if he marks his letter 'Soli', (only for him), only the General will open it and read it first, though he may not be able to answer it himself. This is what makes Jesuit obedience such a powerful and fine-tuned means of governance in the Society of Jesus; it's meant to be a fine balance between commanding and obeying, listening to representation and taking a decision. Of course, there's no higher appeal after the Superior General; the Pope does not entertain such appeals either. God is an option of course, but God was there even before the appeal.

EXPOSURE TO THE WORLD

After our language year in Nashik, in April 1964, we went to De Nobili College, affiliated to Jnana Deep Vidyapeet (JDV) Pune, to study three years of philosophy. Walking from the main gate carrying my baggage, it seemed this was going to be my desert experience: a hot, dry and dusty summer, after my 'winter of discontent' in Nashik, where it was chilly, windy and damp. But my pessimism turned out to be uncalled for.

Here new intellectual challenges opened new horizons. The studies suited me and I found once again acceptance and recognition for which I am still grateful. Some of the professors there accompanied me in a very personal way. When I found some courses very boring and some classes dry as bones, I asked the professor if I could drop out of the class and do a paper instead. He couldn't exempt me from the main courses even though he had noticed me sleepwalking through his classes. But he did exempt me from the minor ones. He trusted I was 'philosophizing' elsewhere!

The challenge of writing the papers for a course was far more work than attending classes and taking an exam, but it was far more rewarding too. I managed to do two papers which really were my introduction to Indian Philosophy. One was on 'The Monotheism of Sankara' on whom our professor, Fr De Smet, had done his dissertation. This appeared in *Indian Ecclesiastical Studies*, the journal published by the Pontifical Oriental Institute of Religious *Studies*, Kottayam. The second was on 'The Pantheism of Ramanuja' and appeared in *Paths Margah*, the academic journal of JDV. I did the same for my course on social ethics with a paper on Aristotle's Politics, 'The Political Philosophy of Aristotle', which appeared in *Paths Margah*, and for our science classes on a critique of methodology, 'Theory and Thesis: A Critique of Method', which appeared in *Indian Ecclesiastical Studies*, now published as *The Indian Journal of Theology*.

Publication was a rather delayed reward but it convinced me that writing was a valuable vocation in our Jesuit intellectual apostolate, and finally launched me on writing as a vocation, but once again a rather delayed one. It was a long meandering journey getting there with many hurdles along the way.

Philosophy was all about asking the right questions, and for me they were especially ones about social issues. I asked the appointed 'spiritual father' of the philosophers how the per diem—the cost per day—of a scholastic could be Rs 5 at the time, when a family of five in India was supposed to live on the same amount. How was this considered poverty? He simply dismissed the question with: 'Brother, your work now is to study, not to ask such questions!'

This was not an answer I expected or could accept, so he went on: 'If you don't believe me, ask the Rector. If not, ask the Provincial. If not, ask the General, and if you don't believe the General leave the Society.'

I was grinning from ear to ear.

'Have you been asked such questions before?' I asked and could see from his reply that the old man was rather hurt. 'Yes, I have told this to many a scholastic and they haven't left the Society; they have left me!'

Good man though he was, he wasn't meant to guide young scholastics. So I wrote to Fr Sopena in Mumbai and he replied honestly: 'I don't have the answer, but don't be afraid and stop asking such questions.' Once again, Fr Sopena had saved my vocation.

In our third year in the philosophate, we staged George Bernard Shaw's *St Joan*. Shaw's take on the papacy is so true even today: 'All reforming popes have been anticlerical, veritable scourges of the clergy.' After all, aren't the prelates and their clerical curias (secretariats) a large part of the Church's bureaucracy that always needs to be reformed and renewed? *Ecclesia semper reformanda, semper renovanda*—Grace builds on nature, it does not negate it.

TAKEN FOR A RIDE

The day after my final comprehensive philosophy exam, I returned to Mumbai and the same afternoon was sent to substitute for the regent* who had left hurriedly to prepare for his university entrance test.

I was given the name of the train station and sent on my way to Vasai, a district to the north of Mumbai across the creek where the Jesuits had an old parish and school. On the suburban train there, I checked with a passenger, who misinformed me and I got off at the wrong suburban station. I hauled my steel trunk, canvas holdall and black umbrella off the train and found there was not a soul on the platform. I was in the middle of a mangrove swamp, all alone.

I had to wait for an hour or so for the next train, and was lucky to be able to find my way to the right station. There I found that the bullock cart from St Michael's Parish School that had been waiting to take me and my luggage had already returned and had to be recalled. It was a long day that ended in the shadows.

The first day Br Errol D'Lima, the exiting regent, introduced me at the morning assembly of the school and the next day hurried off to Mumbai, leaving me to cope. I didn't know my way around St Michael's

* Regency is the period in a Jesuit scholastic's formation when he is assigned to an apostolate as a break in his studies. There is no royalty involved in this 'regency', I assure you. Rather it's testing time for the young Jesuit's resilience. Jesuit folklore on regents is: the end of a scholastic is to be kicked. And even if you didn't turn the other cheek, you got it on both anyway.

School, or where my classroom was. The senior boys had a whale of a time leading me in all the wrong directions and leaving me at the wrong classroom, lost and confused, as they disappeared into the maze of corridors. It was a joke I might have played on someone myself, but this time the joke was on me! Such rugged introductions were par for the course. Nobody noticed, nobody complained. You took it in your stride.

Eventually I found my way around, and after a couple of weeks there, the boys and I did become good friends. Before I left, I took them for a picnic as an investment in their future good behaviour. However, this stint at St Michaels's, was just a dry run for me. The real thing was still some years away. I still had more studies to do.

GO EAST, YOUNG MAN

In the Jesuit world, one year you are on the West coast of India, in Nashik or Vasai; the next you are on the West coast of America. In 1967, I was told I was being sent to study at Gonzaga University, Spokane, in Washington State on the West coast of the USA. There were two scholarships from the university, under a scheme called the Alliance Fellowship, and they had been made available to our province that year. I was assigned one of them because I had done well in my philosophy course. I was not asked where I wanted to go although I did say that I wanted to study sociology;

I saw it as a good background for social engagement. I should have studied economics but there was no one to advise me and sociology seemed the broader option. The only advice I got was: Go East, young man, and that was about the flight to America. The other scholarship went to a younger scholastic, who was to read philosophy. In those days we travelled with a companion—safety in pairs, it was thought! I knew nothing about Gonzaga; I had to find it on the map and point it out to friends. But I was excited to be part of the changes in the post Vatican Church overtaking the West.

We travelled to Spokane over the Pacific. We were innocents abroad, naïve but ready for the adventure. When we landed in Bangkok, the taxi driver spoke only Thai and we ended up being cheated of our meagre travel allowance on the taxi ride from the airport to the Jesuit House, where we were to stop over for a couple of days.

However, we never really wanted for cash; our purse seemed to refill like the widow of Zarephath's 's oil jar and flour bowl! (1 Kings 17:14) Jesuit solidarity stood us in good stead. Everywhere, the Father Minister, the man in charge of the material administrator, would reimburse us generously.

At our next stopover in Tokyo, the street discipline was a culture shock for someone from the chaotic manthan (churning) of Bombay. Everywhere, the Japanese would form orderly queues while we 'junglis' (literarily, jungle inhabitants) from afar would simply break the queue and rush to the front. Not once did anyone stop us or complain. They simply bowed politely and with a trace of contempt for our gwailo (foreign devil) behaviour. In Bangkok I was mistaken for a Thai, in Tokyo for a Japanese, and in Spokane, as an Indian from the nearby 'reservation' in Omak. I might well have had an identity crisis with these multiple mis-ascribed identities.

We arrived in San Francisco on 15 August 1967. In Golden Gate Park, long-haired, gentle young people were inviting everyone to 'wear some flowers in your hair…you're going to meet some gentle people there…' The hippie movement was in full swing. 'Make peace not war', was their soulful motto!

Good Fr Gregory Naik, from the Goa-Poona Province, who was doing a master's in psychology at San Francisco University, was our host. He gave us a wonderful tour of the city. The Golden Gate Bridge, Fisherman's Warf, the cable cars—it's really one of the most beautiful in the US.

It was also the time of the sudden escalation of the Vietnam War that marked a sharp increase in the draft which ultimately forced the conscription of some 500,000 young recruits into the military. The hippie counter-culture demonstrated the growing generation gap between disillusioned, alienated youth, and staid, anomic parents. The free speech movement beginning in the University of California, Berkeley, pointed to the increasing student distrust of campus administration, summed up in student leader Mario Savio's slogan:

'Don't trust anyone over thirty'. It spread rapidly to other campuses, triggering student riots in some major ones.

In such an atmosphere, compulsory conscription into military service for an unwinnable war became so unpopular as to precipitate anti-draft protests across the country. But to the military-industrial complex, the protesters were on the wrong side of the Iron Curtain. (Wisely, India was non-aligned at the time.) Inevitably as graduating students got closer to the military draft lottery, they turned positively hostile to the war.

WINDS OF CHANGE

Meanwhile, the Church was going through terrible spasms with the changes, the aggiornamento (or reorganization), that were being introduced by Vatican Council II. The ancient walls of 'fortress Catholicism' were falling. We believed this was the work of the Holy Spirit, while others felt it was the work of the Devil. This contestation affected the Society and Jesuit formation quite radically. From hot-house closed-in scholasticates (houses of study for scholastics), Jesuit seminary training became more contextualized: the curriculum of studies was made more relevant, scholastics began to engage with the world outside and there was a renewed understanding of mission.

The Gonzaga years were a major influence in my life as a person and a Jesuit. They marked my life in new and wonderful ways. The hippie revolution had begun; the post-Vatican II exodus was sweeping through the Catholic Church and the Society. Gonzaga was a small but vibrant university which was actively and creatively adjusting to changing times. There was so much freedom but I rarely, if ever, saw my Jesuit companions abuse it. I realized too that I could find a life for myself outside the Society and even the Church, but I also experienced the joy and limits of human intimacy. I had to deepen my convictions and renew my commitments, undergoing a personal aggiornamento myself.

An atheist friend of mine from India presented me with an alternative challenge: why are you wasting your time and talents in the Society of Jesus and the Catholic Church? Surely there are better things you could do! This forced me to consider whether I would be spending too much intellectual and emotional energy working against the structures and strictures of organizations that had taken hundreds of years to make. Yet, much of what I became later began then.

CHEAP AND COSTLY FAITH

The only card-carrying Communist on the Gonzaga campus was Nick Braun, who was also a friend. He was working his way through college as a busboy on the night shift downtown, walking almost an hour each way in sub-freezing winter temperatures because he couldn't get any other job. At the time I did not realize how much courage it took for him to stand up for his convictions; nor did I have any idea that he might be 'dangerous' to know. Then one day while I was sitting alone in the cafeteria with some books, two large men in trench coats approached me with a studied casualness.

'May we join you?' one of them asked. I indicated that they were welcome and they joined my table. They did not introduce themselves but asked if I knew Nick Braun. I said I did. They started asking me details of my association with Nick: how long I had known him, how well. I suddenly realized where this was going and asked why they wanted to know. They weren't very forthcoming so I declined to say anything more. We never got as far as discussing the Vietnam War but I suppose they smelled the pink stain. For with the Left, I had questioned the war. Spending 30 billion dollars that year on a war to protect some 12 million Vietnamese from the Reds and just one billion on developmental aid for the rest of the world, didn't make much sense to me, no matter the hypothetical 'domino effect'.

When I asked the other scholastics what these men in the trench coats was all about, no one seemed surprised. 'Don't you know? That's the FBI!' one of them said. I was completely ignorant of such surveillance.

One night I called Nick over to Bea House—the scholastics' residence on campus—for a sandwich and a beer. We discussed our common friend Karl through the night until it was nearly four a.m.

Finally, to end an impasse between Church and Party, I asked him, 'If Marx were proved wrong, would you change your mind about him?'

His reply was simple: 'Can't be.'

I persisted, 'Per impossible, would you?'

After a long deep pause, he said softly, 'Yes, I would.'

But at the door, as he was getting into his coat, he swung around and shot the same question at me, 'And what about you? If Jesus were proved to be wrong, what would you do?'

I found myself saying almost the same thing. That it could not happen.

He persisted in mirroring me, 'If…per impossible…'

I found myself fumbling for words.

Like a flash of lightning, I realized what Dietrich Bonhoeffer meant when he talked about the difference between costly faith and cheap grace. The first demands your whole life; the second offers a shallow faith in a comfort zone and without challenge. Illumination may come in a variety of ways.

THE HIPPIE

At Gonzaga I made many beautiful and lasting friendships, with Jesuits and others, men and women, hippies and potheads. Sometimes I was even mistaken for a hippie pothead with my shoulder-length hair and the sun-rise pendant I wore around my neck.

There was a counter-culture pattern among my friends as well. Other than Nick, there was the 6-feet-6-inches-tall basketball player and Black Power activist, Joe McNair; Alessandro Falassi, an Italian who later became a professor at the University of Sienna; and Mary Clark, later a campus minister in Grand Rapids, Michigan who has been a lifelong friend. Then there was Alice Ray who became a Gandhian of sorts, and in 2018, did the Dandi March in reverse, working her way from the seashore to the ashram. This was to underscore the importance of and the commitment of their group of like-minded peace-activists to Gandhi's satyagraha. She even visited me at the Indian Social Institute, New Delhi. She had come to set up a child training programme for migrant Afghan children.

Among the unforgettable Jesuits I met there was Fr Van Christoph, my faculty advisor. He was a rugged, rough and tough American with a heart larger than his big frame. He would proudly claim that while studying in New Orleans he had been mistaken for a Black and told to sit at the back of the bus!

He had once scolded me rather heatedly: 'Rudi, you're late. You have no business keeping me like this waiting for an appointment *you* made.'

And before I could make the standard tired claim that by Indian standards I was only politely late, he went on, 'Now, what was it you wanted to discuss?'

Time management was one of my early inculturation experiences, coming as I did from a country where in some of our villages, time was still told by the position of the sun.

At Gonzaga University, I had become quite a hippie myself. I generally 'hung out' with the 'kids'. My companion scholastics at Bea House would tease me: Rudi is a 'man for others', as good Jesuits ought to be, not one for us.

My first summer break, I took a $126 sixty-day Greyhound Bus pass, 'travel as you please', from coast to coast and north to south, covering at least some 10,000 miles. I enjoyed Jesuit hospitality wherever I stopped overnight, introducing myself as from the Bombay Mission. And after fifty-four hours on a Greyhound bus, (say, New Orleans to Los Angeles) I really needed a bed, just to relish the feeling of the steady ground under my feet.

I saw a vast and beautiful country, but where the human habitat was so similar: the hotels, and motels, the skyscrapers and log cabins. Everyone even spoke the same language, except for the variations in their accents. And I felt so proud of the diversity of India, where from diet to dress, from language to lifestyles, the scenario changed over and over with the miles.

HOMEWARD BOUND

In my final weeks at Gonzaga, I was in a great hurry to finish writing my MA thesis, the final requirement for the degree. I would work through the night and cat-nap in the day. By the beginning of the summer of 1969, I was ready to return home. The other scholastic who had come with me had left the Jesuits and was now having a hard time working the night shift to pay his way through college as a layman. He noticed I had suddenly become very concerned for him. He once said to me: 'Rudi, you weren't this nice to me when I was a Jesuit.' How could I tell him I had distanced myself from him then because his naiveté as a companion from India embarrassed me no end? But now his present need spoke to me louder than my earlier embarrassment. I was trying to make it up to him rather late in the day, because I felt guilty for not having done this before. And truth to tell, I still feel guilty and ashamed of this lapse on my part.

Gonzaga and Spokane have stamped my life and entwined it with those of many others. I experienced many beautiful people who have left their footprints on my soul. Leaving was a real wrench. At my farewell Mass with student friends and Jesuit companions, there was more silence than sharing as I told them how in India when someone is leaving, we say: 'Come again'. And the appropriate response is: 'Yes, I'm coming back.'

Little wonder our railway stations are so crowded, not with passengers but with friends and family and well-wishers seeing off their near and dear ones—trains being the most affordable and favoured means of long-distance travel.

Early next morning a few friends came to see me off as I flew out of Spokane on a cold winter morning in February 1969 almost two years after landing there.

John Denver's 'Leaving on a Jet Plane' was playing in the deserted airport lounge. The song brought tears of gratitude for all that had been and all I could dream. It still echoes in my head: 'Cause I'm leavin' on a jet plane / Don't know when I'll be back again…'

But as I told my friends at the Mass for my farewell:

Goodbye

I'm sorry to leave, but happy to go;
I have places to visit
and things to do
tasks to complete,
and people to meet.

I still reconnect with Gonzaga whenever I meet the people I once was together with there, as I often do with Mary T, when I have visited with her in her home, or when she came to see me in St Louis in September 2014.

TEACHER OR CLOWN

In the summer of 1969, I was back in India in the nitty-gritty, hurly-burly of Mumbai city for my formal regency at St Xavier's College. My earlier stint at the school in Manickpur was as a pro temp substitute. This was for real now. Teaching as a young scholastic in St Xavier's College was quite an experience. I returned to India with an MA in sociology, to teach the subject at the college as a regent at the request of the college principal, Fr Edward D'Cruz. He had been on sabbatical for a semester at Gonzaga where I had been doing my Master's degree and there he came to know me well. My regency at Xavier's was just a year, but a very eventful one for me. I was the only scholastic, living in a community of much older, and sometimes rather 'over-revered' Fathers. I was mostly referred to not by name, but by the impersonal title: 'the scholastic'!

I had to consciously decide to be myself, not just their 'scholastic'. But if it wasn't for the support of the Rector, Fr Parmanda Divarkar, a truly great and authentic Jesuit, I wouldn't have survived there. The community was still adjusting to Vatican II. With all the tensions and dissensions this entailed, a non-conforming scholastic could easily become a scapegoat.

This was my first experience of teaching undergrads as a young scholastic and it was a baptism of fire, my first avatar as a teaching clown at Xavier's. We weren't in the habit of wearing our cassocks to class at the time. On my first day to make sure I was in the right lecture room, I entered hesitantly and asked the girl on the first bench, 'Is this the sociology class?'

Waving me to a seat she said, 'Yeah, sit down somewhere. The prof hasn't come as yet.'

I replied, 'I'm the prof.'

She looked me up and down and turned to class and yelled, 'Hey guys, this chap says he's our prof!'

The whole class started cheering. Or were they jeering? I was too nervous to tell. Not the best way to begin a teaching career, much less a teaching vocation, I can assure you.

I suppose the problem was that I looked younger than my twenty-eight years and there wasn't that much of a difference between me and them. That wasn't exactly a good thing in the situation but it could not be helped. If students took me as one of them, I had to find another teacher-student relationship with them. That was my challenge. There were no 'ID' cards for teachers. You just had to look your part and play it, much like marriage in common law. I taught the first and last year undergrad arts students. There was no junior college in Bombay then, since the Kothari Commission's formula—ten years of secondary school and two of higher secondary school or junior college as it is termed in Mumbai—had not yet come into effect. Things settled down and became more manageable once they began to see me as more friend than teacher.

CHAPLAIN CHARLIE

I was made the facilitator of the Catholic Students Union (CSU). This appointment was actually for a full-fledged priest who could act as chaplain. But the anomaly was conveniently ignored because none of the older priests wanted anything to do with the CSU since it had developed a reputation for being difficult and rebellious. So 'the scholastic' was dumped with it. I decided that the only way to deal with these rowdies was to become one of them—I mean to become their companion and not their 'chaplain'. If I had tried to play the latter role, they might have nicknamed me 'Charlie'; and that would have locked me into a clown's role for the rest of the year, which isn't exactly what a beginning teacher looks for. 'Rudi' with all its derivatives was quite enough. The title 'Father' made me shrink. I didn't feel like one to all the 'hulks' and 'beauties' on campus!

CSU AND BHARATANATYAM

The effect of Vatican Council II, as I remember, was a tectonic shift in the ground on which we were all standing, for clergy and laity alike. When I was growing up, we did not see the priest's face at Holy Mass. He would turn his back on us and address God. Now the altars were turned to face the people, many priests could not take this new position, this eye contact. One of the senior priests began celebrating his Mass in the sacristy of the Jesuit chapel of the nearby St Xavier's High School. (He was thus eating a sacred meal, a commemorating of Jesus's own last Passover supper with his disciples, on his own and alone, in complete contravention of the original intent of the Eucharist. But this did not occur to him, it would seem.) Others couldn't understand con-celebration in which more than one priest celebrates the holy meal in commemoration of the Last Supper Christ ate on earth; they said it made them feel like 'altar boys'. In other words, they had an ego problem. And altar girls were, of course, a scandal. What starts at the altar may not end there, they kept saying.

Fr Parmanda accompanied the community gently but firmly through the ups and downs, the back and forth of what was at times a frustrating process. Coming from the freewheeling liturgies at Gonzaga, this was another 'culture shock', in reverse!

That Christmas, the CSU had organized a Bharatanatyam offertory dance for midnight Mass to the tune of a popular Hindi hymn, 'Tera Noor' (Your Light). In 1969, inculturation was still controversial in Bombay. So I was careful to get permission from the Rector (who was in favour), and informed the Archbishop's House office (which was neutral). At the Mass there was a little protest by some 'out-standing' local Catholics at the back of the congregation. It was hardly noticed by the rest but commented on in the local conservative Catholic press and by some outraged, fuddy-duddy Jesuits at the next community meeting.

One of pompous old Fathers solemnly queried: 'Who gave permission for this? How dare the scholastic do this on his own?'

When the Rector said he had given permission, the Father started fumbling and mumbling. I thought I must now stand up for the students, stop this grandstanding by this grand old man and put him in his place.

I looked him in the eye and said, 'You haven't helped at all in the chaplaincy; never a Mass or service for the students. As a not-yet-ordained minister, I had to improvise it all. You have no moral right to ask me for an account. I simply refuse to be accountable to one like you.' His silence said the rest. However, the students saw me as playing for their team and felt we had won that round. But of course, I knew there would be others to come. Stubborn old men don't give up easily.

This Bharatnatyam caper got the CSU into enormous extramural trouble. The old Jesuits in the community and the old Christians in the neighbourhood were outraged at this intrusion of the alien into the sacred liturgy. Even the local Catholic press got into the act: the walls of their tradition, their fortress, were being brought down. But Fr Parmanda stood by me and the students. In his inimitable way, he explained this liturgical experiment as being merely 'a rhythmic interpretation of a vernacular hymn'! This calmed the storm though no one quite understood what it meant, so no one contested what Fr Parmanda had said. He had the knack of confusing things for the better! At least it assuaged the vocal opposition by many who hadn't been there at that Christmas midnight liturgy in the first place.

TEACHING AS AN ART FORM

Fr John Macia, who was in the sociology department of St Xavier's for many years, would say: 'Students learn more in the canteen than in the classroom.' His subject was social anthropology. In the classroom, he did not so much lecture as pantomime the subject matter. Things came alive for the students as a large-framed Jesuit priest began doing a tribal war dance that shook the classroom. They were first amazed. Then they laughed. And they relaxed and learned lessons they would never forget.

Good examination results? That did not matter to Father Macia. He knew he had left them with an indelible store of knowledge about the commonality of the human experience. He had not taught them anything; they had learned it on their own, watching him with eyes wide and receptive rather than focussed on filling pages like the stenographers we breed across the country in lecture rooms.

With all its ups and downs, frustrations and hopes, in my first experience as a teacher and later confirmed, I'm quite sure I learnt more than I taught. My one take away from my teaching was this: the most lasting impact on young people is the personal relationship they develop with a role model. And that happens less inside the classroom than outside. The classroom merely opens a door; accompanying the student must go beyond that, if it's to a make a real difference.

There are three factors that students take into account when it comes to evaluating classroom teaching: covering the subject-matter assigned to the course; a relaxed but orderly classroom; and relating the subject to their world outside the class. Furthermore, if they like you as a person, they generally like you as a teacher and vice versa. In other words, being a nice person is more important for students than being just a good lecturer.

A good teacher learns to combine the pragmatic and the idealistic without compromising either. The pragmatic teacher says I can take you to the water but I cannot make you drink. The idealistic teacher believes that it is her duty to rouse interest and curiosity so that they will explore the terrain and find the spring of water themselves and even excel their teacher. A true guru would wish for his shishyas to excel him (Sadguru shishyaat icchet paraajayam), for 'the excellence of the disciples enhances the fame of the teacher' (shishyaprakrshaa yashase gurupranam).

FEELING THE MYSTIQUE

In our Eastern tradition, to 'take darshan' is to be present. It is presence that changes us not mere articulation: 'feeling' rather than learning, i.e, entering 'into' not just 'conceptualizing' the divine mysteries.

So in 1970, when I went to De Nobili College, affiliated to JDV, once again, this time for my theological studies, it was 'to take darshan' of the divine. I enjoyed this more than philosophy, because I felt it brought me into the mainstream of my mission in the Church, and it was challenging to find a critical space there, especially after Vatican II.

Some of the professors who taught me were real giants. Fr Joseph Neuner had been a peritus (expert advisor) to the Indian bishops at Vatican II. His classes were monotonous, but now and then he would come up with a gem that made it all worthwhile. I remember him teaching us how the Council of Chalcedon (AD 451) defined for us Jesus Christ as 'true God and true man' to settle all controversies on Christology in the Church. So we start with one mystery 'Jesus' and explain it by two others, 'man' and 'God'! This was for me a path breaking insight that changed my approach to theological learning. Sacred mysteries can't be conceptualized in dogmatic definitions, even ones by Ecumenical Councils. Rather they are signposts that mark the path one must follow to enter deeper into the mystery.

Like all religious language, mysteries are necessarily articulated in symbolic language. And we need a strategy to unpack them. To turn them into formulae and repeat these ad nauseam betrays the mystery. 'Belief' replaces 'faith', dogma dismisses mystery. But if we look at the mysteries as invitations to enter into the experience of the mystery with our hearts, we are suddenly elevated into another plane of experience. To conceptualize with our heads is to try and dissect the beauty of a butterfly with a hacksaw. The beauty dies first; the tools are the wrong ones; and the end is disaster.

Fr Neuner was a man far ahead of his times. In the 1940s, interned as a prisoner of war in Dehradun in the Himalayan foothills, he and a handful of Jesuit scholastics, German and Austrian missionaries in British

India, began teaching themselves theology from the few textbooks available to them. In the 1950s when De Nobili College was being built, he had suggested that the scholastics be housed in multiple small residences, sharing common facilities. He was shouted down. The other Jesuits saw anarchy in this idea. How would they ensure silence, discipline! Now of course, this sounds like a silly argument made by control freaks. Today, the disaggregated model is par for the course. But De Nobili still stands with its some 300-odd rooms that could be a military barrack or a state prison!

In the evening of his life, I remember telling him how disturbed I was with the notification from the Congregation for Doctrine and Faith, *Dominus Iesus* (2000)*. He leaned over and in a loud, hoarse whisper said to me: 'Monophysitism, brother, monophysitism.' That was an early Christian heresy against which Chalcedon inveighed against. (Monophysitism maintained that Jesus Christ had only a single divine nature that appeared in human form. This had been discredited hundreds of years ago and was suddenly resurfacing in this extraordinary document. One needs an especial hermeneutic to save its orthodoxy.) At the time Fr Neuner was ninety-eight years old and still keenly involved in the theological issues of the day. He died at a hundred and two years!

Another Jesuit there who inspired me was Fr George

---

* *Dominus Iesus* is a declaration by the Congregation for the Doctrine of the Faith, approved in a Plenary meeting of the Congregation and signed by its then Prefect, Joseph Cardinal Ratzinger, later Pope Benedict XVI.

Soares, an extraordinarily brilliant teacher and radical scripture scholar. He would draw a word picture of his lecture as he went along and leave a perfect summary on the blackboard. If only we had smartphones then to click those! He showed us how to read the 'option for the poor' into the Gospel and find there a social-class analysis for those times, which we could apply to ours. George Soares died in a tragic road accident, just when he retired from formal teaching and was preparing to work on his opus magnum, *The Dharma of Jesus*, an indigenous interpretation to the New Testament.

Among the many Rectors I had at De Nobili, one I deeply admired and loved was Fr Jose Ugarte, a Spaniard, who in the 1930s during the Spanish Civil War, had joined the French Jesuit province, then responsible for the Madurai mission in India. He was an unpretentious man, yet totally self-possessed and at ease with himself. De Nobili College was one of the largest scholasticates in the Society and one of the most diverse in language, ethnicity and nationality at the time.

Fr Ugarte transformed it from a large anonymous community into small manageable living groups each to be accompanied by a faculty member. The opposition of some old professors was unfortunate. Of course, the system was not perfect but it did help humanize a large crowd into groups of companions. It was a turning point for the house, and the 'living groups' format he put in place still prevails there and has been taken over by most large scholasticates elsewhere.

The living group a few of us formed was deliberately heterogeneous: one of us was a 'protestant' of sorts, another a 'catholic', with a small 'c', and others of assorted marginal orthodoxies. What we lacked was a true-blue heretic but even without one the clash of ideas made the study of theology an exciting time.

These interchanges—was it dialogue or was it merely debate, I still cannot be sure—would go on late into the night and even until the small hours of the morning, with a little help from instant coffee. Once we even had Raimondo Panikkar, the internationally known polyglot join us, courtesy Fr Francis DeSa, the Indologist on the JDV faculty. Panikkar would treat every person and question with respect and seriousness; he always answered more than one asked.

For our out-reach ministry, a group of us worked with the college students in the town. There were five of us in the coordinating team. We organized retreats and recollections, study workshops and live-in renewals. This began in the first year of my theology course and carried through the three years there.

While studying theology too I preferred writing papers instead of attending lectures, and wrote two of them. 'Covenant Theology' was published in *Indian Ecclesiastical Studies* and 'The Uniqueness of Jesus Christ' in *Indian Theological Studies*.

DISCERNING WITH ONE'S HEART

In my second year of theology, I made a thirty-day retreat with Fr Tony de Mello* to discern what the orientation of my evangelical life should be. The choice was between being a Jesuit priest or a Jesuit brother, then considered slightly lower in the peking order, which of course no one admitted existed.

I had already seen many fall into the soft option of the clerical career, rather than choosing the rigours of the Jesuit religious life without the support of clerical status. I didn't want that to happen to me. Which would be the 'more excellent offering', the 'magis', which St Ignatius repeatedly urges the retreatant to make in the *Spiritual Exercises*? I had to tussle with the Rector of the Athenaeum, Fr Herbert Alphonso, who was reluctant to let me off classes. Finally I had to pretend to be on the verge of a spiritual crisis. Of course, he didn't believe me but he saw that I was serious and so let me go.

Tony, already a national and later an international figure, was a true guru, as gentle as he was firm and I came out just the same only more so, with one difference; he introduced me to Buddhist prayer, Satipatthana and Vipassana. Ever since this mindfulness has been the basis of my meditation and prayer, something I've always fallen back on.

---

* Anthony de Mello, also known as Tony de Mello, was an Indian Jesuit priest and psychotherapist. A spiritual teacher, writer and public speaker, de Mello wrote several books on spirituality and hosted numerous spiritual retreats and conferences.

He told me to lay aside the issue I had brought for discernment and wait for it to emerge in my prayer. On the twenty-eighth day of the retreat, I asked Tony, 'What about the issue I had come to discern? We haven't referred to it at all.'

He asked, 'Did it come up in your prayer?' Honestly? It hadn't.

'Forget about it then,' he concluded.

I understood he was asking me to walk my faith. With this came the realization that discerning is really a matter of listening to my heart, not just thinking with my head. Perhaps I was living too much in my head.

And so the next year I happily went on for my ordination retreat in January 1973 at the restored Jesuit residence attached to the Basilica of the Bom Jesus in Old Goa, where the mausoleum of St Francis Xavier is. There we were ordained deacons, the first step to priestly ordination.

SNEHASADAN

Scholastics in their third year of theology were allowed to spend a year living as a group outside De Nobili College in a nearby slum. I was keen on doing this, but in my third year I could not find any group companions. So I asked and was allowed to live in a Jesuit ashram across town in the heart of the old city of Pune where two other older Jesuit priests had set up an ashram for inter-religious dialogue. I became an off-campus student. I was not required to attend classes but once a week I had to visit De Nobili College and check with the teachers on the work assigned to me.

Snehasadan (house of friendship) had an ashram lifestyle: sleeping on the floor, squatting on the ground for work and vegetarian meals, etc. We ate the midday meal in a khanavalay (eatery) nearby in the town. Only tea, coffee, bread and soup were available at home. I would supplement my protein intake with peanuts from street vendors from the little pocket money we scholastics were given. And truly it was the one time in my Jesuit life that I experienced hunger! But halfway through another Jesuit priest, Fr Rui de Menezes, joined us. He was a linguist who spoke Tulu, Konkani, Marathi, Gujarati and English, with regional accents too, besides the classical and biblical languages, i.e., Latin, Greek, Hebrew, as also modern European ones, like German, Spanish, French, Italian. He was appointed to the ashram as the administrator; he upgraded and modernized the ashram, just before I was called back to De Nobili by the Rector to study for my final exams.

The acharya of the ashram was Fr Matthew Lederle, whom I got to know rather well during my time there. He had ended his military service in World War II as a seventeen-year-old German paratrooper defending airports on the Russian front. He was tough as steel and gentler than a feather, a living illustration of St Francis de Sales' maxim: 'There is nothing as strong as true gentleness; there's nothing as gentle as real strength.'

A German television company had asked him to do a preliminary survey for the documentary they were planning on Buddhist holy sites in north India and other holy places around Rishikesh in the Himalayas. He invited me to join him on the trip, scheduled during the vacation after my exams and of course, I jumped at the offer. This was my chance to discover the India of the Buddhists and rishis, an India I hardly knew.

BODHGAYA

We started at Patna and among the places we visited was the dialogue centre at Bodhgaya, then a nascent Christian initiative as I recall. We paid homage to the Bodhi Tree, in the Mahabodhi Temple Complex and rested in its ambience. We stopped by the Deer Park where the Buddha had preached his first sermon. I carry in my mind startling images of the massive brick ruins of Nalanda University, which at its peak in the 11th century AD, housed some 11,000 residential monks. What must the place have been like when once it was bustling in full session?

On the long, hot train ride across the Gangetic plain from Patna to Rishikesh, Matthewji, as he was called, told me of his war experiences. He was on the retreating Eastern Front and the German soldiers were trying to make it to the Allied lines in the West. To be taken by the Russians meant immediate deportation to Siberian labour camps. He managed to get as far as the

Elbe and swam across to be taken by the Americans, who were rather arbitrary with POWs. You could be severely punished if caught smuggling in a loaf of bread or let off with a laugh. The British, however, had a sense of fair play—always easier when you're winning than when you're losing.

RISHIKESH

In the cool foothills where the river Ganga broke into the plains, Rishikesh was a pilgrimage centre. A bath there was considered especially auspicious, washing away all of one's sins! We took a dip in the river there and found it wonderfully refreshing, washing away the heat and dust of the plains. The evening aarti on the river with the little lamps floating downstream, while the *Ram-dhun*, the traditional bhajan, sung with such devotion added enchantment to the scene. Today Lord Rama has been politicized. 'Jai Shri Ram' has been turned into a war cry which emphasizes only one aspect of a truly multifaceted and complex personality; we only hear of Ram Raudra (the warlike) and nothing about Ram Soumya (the gentle), Ram the Maryada Purush, the complete human being.

We rested at the Shivananda Ashram and set off by bus to Rishikesh the next morning. It was a nerve-racking experience. Only the week earlier one of these converted Tata-Mercedes-Benz trucks had crashed 5,000 feet into the valley below. There had been no survivors. But the drivers were undaunted. Just when they had raced around a curve a foot from the edge of the ravine below, they would turn to the bewildered passengers, eyes off the road, grin triumphantly, twirling their mustachios on both sides, hands off the wheel.

Crossing another vehicle on the outside was terrifying. An occasional boulder rolling onto the road was quickly blasted away by the army. These border roads had to be kept open, since they were just twenty miles from the Chinese border.

The real obstacle that caused a long delay was an Indian police border guard who wouldn't accept Matthewji's Indian passport as proof of citizenship until he had conferred with his neighbouring commander. Evidently, he had never seen a passport before and didn't know what it meant. There was vigilance in the town as well but the army officer there acknowledged the validity of Matthewji's papers and let us pass.

BADRINATH

We stayed overnight in town and unfortunately Matthewji had to return urgently to Shivananda Ashram for an important meeting with Swami Chidananda. I was determined to see the fabled ice Shivling so I soldiered on. It was freezing when I reached the cave at 10,000 feet; there was still snow on the shadow side of the mountain, though it was July now.

But when I looked into the cave, the ice Shivaling

didn't seem to do much honour to Shiva. It hadn't been cold for long enough for it to form. And with global warming this is getting commoner; some years ago the lingam had to be built up with pack-ice. Was this the right thing to do? I don't know. To my mind, true devotees don't need to see with their eyes; they have hearts to internalize the 'darshan'.

The bus ride back was more memorable than the one up. Due to the recent accidents, a limit had been placed on the number of passengers per bus. A speed limit was evidently unenforceable on lonely mountain roads. But a passenger seat limit could be checked before a bus left the terminal gate. In our bus there was one extra passenger. A recount confirmed this and a poor mendicant woman squatting on the floor was identified as the single extra. She couldn't afford a ticket, she said. So the other passengers contributed to buy her one. But due to the recent restrictions on numbers the bus conductor said there was no place for her. She naturally thought she was being played around with and simply refused to get off. 'Am I in anyone's way?' she demanded to know.

The bus conductor insisted the police would stop them at the outer gate of the bus terminal and force the vehicle to return and perhaps even arrest him. No one had the heart to force the poor old lady off the bus. So, seeing a sadhu there among the passengers, they turned him into the scapegoat. 'You're supposed to be a sadhu, a renunciate, so you should give up your seat!'

He was furious, 'None of you helped me when I was struggling on the way up and now you want me to surrender my seat?' And he roundly cursed the passengers as he got off. They were so frightened by this ill omen before a dangerous bus ride that they hastily called him back and put him on the next bus. The incident took over an hour, so the next bus was not far behind. With a little adjustment all were accommodated. 'Adjust karo, adjust karo' (adjust a little, adjust a little) is a survival strategy in this crowded, disorderly country. So with all satisfied, we began our descent and reached Rishikesh safe and dry.

Then we descended to the summer heat and dust of the sprawling plains of India.

SACRED ANOINTING

On 7th April 1973, seven of us were ordained presbyters (priests) in St Peter's, Bandra, Mumbai. Six Jesuits: Lisbert and his brother Gilbert D'Souza, Berkie D'Souza, Aloysius Murzello and I for Bombay province; Ornellas Coutinho for Gujarat; and one seminarian, John D'Mello, for Bombay Archdiocese.

At the door of Church, my mother tearfully blessed me, crossing my forehead, just as she had when I had joined the novitiate some thirteen years ago, when she first could see that 'faint outline of a man of God'. By now I had come to realize that my mother's love would always be a bit anxious even in celebration. As she sent me to the altar, she finally was giving me up to God. This was the first time I felt she had really accepted her son as a Jesuit priest. For me, her blessing was as sacred as the imposition of the bishop's hands later that evening. Some years later I wrote this for her:

Living in Trust

I go with gratitude and good cheer
with a sense of incompleteness in my heart
that leaves a still unspoken, sadness in my soul
and I'm wondering where it comes from.
For it is not a sense of closure I seek
But rather a feeling of openness I long for.

Is it perhaps I don't trust enough?
For if trust makes me open
then I know I'm too closed!
This has always been a sensitive issue—
because I have disillusioned many who once trusted
    me—
and a painful one too.
I have felt how hard one hits
the bottom of the pit
when one is let down!

But please believe it is not you I mistrust—
or else my love would be so hollow.
Mine is really a more impersonal,
a deeper and more sinful lack of faith!

If I seize the initiative
want to be in control,
if I won't let go, won't go with the flow,
if I organize and plan
and plot and scheme,
calculate and anticipate,

if I worry and fret and nervously sweat,
isn't it because I'm overestimating my power
and overextending my responsibilities?
Isn't this a not-so-subtle arrogance
that ultimately amounts to a mistrust of God?

Perhaps you will understand then,
why I so overreach myself
and stretch my spirit to the breaking point.
For only when I'm broken and bruised,
abandoned and lost,
when I cry Eloi, Eloi*, only then
can his power be made manifest in my weakness
and his trust in me heal my mistrust of you.

I hope you will understand
What so few do—
So few who can really call me by my name—
And if you can't
Who will deflate my arrogance or lift me up when
I'm down
And make my lesson in trust
A little less painful than it has been till now?

(12 November 1976)

* For 'Eloi eloi, lama sabachthani'. (My God, my God, why have you abandoned me!) These are the words Christ spoke as He died on the cross; they are also the opening lines of Psalm 23.

SECOND TEACHING AVATAR

Towards the end of my theology course, I was assigned to St Xavier's College and asked to do an MA in psychology to replace the Jesuit taking early retirement and moving on. But why could there not be a layperson in psychology and a Jesuit in the economics department, which at the time was the more important one? Well then, I was told you can do an MA in economics as well!

This was becoming bizarre. Eventually, I managed to get permission to complete my sociological studies since I didn't want to lose the momentum I already had in the subject. I taught sociology for a year to prove myself to the new principal and to firm up my pedagogic skills in the subject.

By this time, the Kothari Commission's recommendation (Ten years in school, two in junior college and three in the degree college) was in force. I was put to teach the two ends of the adolescence spectrum: the First Year of Junior College (FYJC) students, who had just come out of school with only the fuzziest notion of sociology; and the First Year BA class, many of whom took sociology as a soft option, an add on before they dropped it and took the subject of their choice for the final year. My job, as I saw it, was to change a few minds about the value and importance of sociology.

In my second brief teaching avatar at Xavier's, I

believe I had developed a little more gravitas. I was older and felt wiser. It helped that the Jesuit community took me more seriously: I wasn't a scholastic now but an ordained priest. However, after a three-year break, it was like beginning anew with the students. Preparing my lectures was still hard work, lecturing twenty hour-long classes per week to a hundred-plus talkative teenagers without a microphone still left me with 'teacher's throat' by the end of term. And correcting hundreds of exam scripts took away most of my vacation. The year flew by and I had to leave for my doctoral studies to equip myself for my third avatar in teaching.

VISA HURDLES

I began my studies at the University of Chicago in 1974, with a scholarship from MISEREOR, the German charity that was quite big here in India. But getting a student visa for the US had become a hazardous process because of the steep increase in applicants—for student visas in particular. At Bombay you stood in long queues outside the consulate in the open, rain or shine and waited your turn. When the quota for the day was over, the door shut. You had to come back the next day and do it over again. I went very early in the morning, waited for hours and managed to get in just before the doors were shut for the day.

The interview was fine, and then just before

stamping my visa, the vice-consul asked me: 'You're not planning to stay on, are you?'

This was an unfair insinuation. Did he think I was an illegal immigrant risk? Or that everyone here was falling over to get into that 'city on the hill'?

I was so annoyed I looked him in the eye and replied slowly, 'And why would I want to do that?' He could have rejected my visa, though I don't think I would have regretted my answer. But he sat up and actually apologized, 'I'm sorry, I realize there are some questions we must not ask certain persons.' Decent of him to do so but he should have known better in the first place.

TORONTO ON THE WAY

My student visa secure, I decided to break journey visiting friends and family in Toronto. It was all in the same ticket anyway. Strangely, the Canadian immigration official checked all my US papers as I was entering Canada, even personal letters, and quizzed me for almost an hour. Finally, he wanted to open the sealed I-20 student-visa form from the American Consulate in Bombay and I had to stop him dead.

'Oh no, you don't,' I said sharply and he looked at me startled.

'You can't do that; it's clearly marked: "To be opened by United States Immigration Officials only".' I think he was a bit taken aback. He must have realized he had overextended his brief but tried to recoup.

'The US immigration officer is just down the corridor,' he said.

By now I was really upset, so I shot back, 'Then let's go there together—now.' Suddenly he stopped pulling rank and became very polite. My school friend, Munawar Baig, who was waiting outside, must have thought I was being repatriated as an unwanted alien. When I told him of the little contretemps I had had inside, he shook his head in disbelief.

My luggage hadn't arrived with me in Toronto, even after a two-hour wait at the airport, so Munawar helped me file a complaint and we left. The next morning I called from his home to enquire and was told that in a couple of days I would be informed when I could come and pick it up at the airport.

Munawar grabbed the phone and said crisply in an unmistakably professional tone: 'I'm Fr Heredia's lawyer. If the luggage doesn't arrive here by 11.00 a.m. tomorrow, you'll hear from me.' Then he put the receiver down, gently but firmly. I gaped at him and he winked.

'You aren't a lawyer,' I said.

'He doesn't know that,' he replied.

Sure enough, it worked. What I didn't realize was that I could have demanded $200 as compensation at the time. As a student who was just setting out on a long haul, I could really have used the money too.

Besides the usual hearty camaraderie when old friends and long-lost relatives meet, the best advice I got in Toronto was from someone who had studied at the

University of Chicago: 'remember, a good dissertation is a finished dissertation'. I realized how important this was at the very start when I got to the university. I found that approximately 40 per cent of PhD candidates ended up as 'ABD' (All but Dissertation!). So my priority was not to write the last word on the subject, but the final one of my thesis.

MEMORABLE ENTRY

Munawar wanted my entry into the US of A to be really memorable, and so it was. We drove from Toronto over the Friendship Bridge, across the Niagara Falls into Buffalo: Munawar, his wife Kousar, and my sister Selena. The other three had no problem—Munawar and Kousar were resident Canadians, and Selena, a returning student. But I had to present all my student-visa papers to the immigration officer again.

He looked over them and asked, 'So you are a Jesuit, one of those troublemakers?' Evidently some Jesuit in Boston had recently given grief to the Cardinal Archbishop there. Very apologetically, I ventured to say that there are some 30,000 of us and we're all not the same. He shot back, 'How would I know? I'm not one of them. Ask that guy at the back there; he's a dropout.'

I suppose he meant an ex-seminarian. And from the back I heard, 'Oh, but then we didn't go around with our girlfriends.'

I turned around to see Munawar's wife standing by just in case. So I lamely said, 'But she's my best friend's wife.'

Only to be put in my place with, 'Oh haven't we heard that one before!'

I'm not sure this rather traditional and conservative Muslim lady was cued into what was going on. But this was getting messier and messier, so I decided to just keep quiet as he stamped my visa with a laugh and I was through.

CHICAGO, HERE I COME!

And so in the autumn of 1974, I began work on my doctorate. MISEREOR paid for my tuition on the condition that I work for five years in India after completing my degree, which I was planning to do in any case. For my per diem, the Jesuit Province Mission Office found me a local parish where I served as a resident priest to cover my board and lodging. I've never regretted either: the rigorous intellectual demands of the life of the mind at the University of Chicago that lifted me up into the world of ideas, or the down-to-earth experience of a blue-collar parish, St Bridget's at Bridgeport, across the canal from the Westside ghetto.

Once, on hearing that I was returning from a university class at 10 p.m., an old parishioner was alarmed: 'That's dangerous. Why are you going to that university in middle of the ghetto on the South-side. Why don't you go to *our* university on the North-side?'

He meant Loyola University, right on Lake Michigan where on 'a clear day you can see forever' almost across to Michigan. How could I explain the difference between the University of Chicago and Loyola University? So I just obfuscated with, 'Well, I got admission there, you see.'

He looked sympathetic—probably thought I hadn't made the grade with Loyola. Actually I didn't want to go to a Jesuit university since I would come back to teach in a Jesuit college. I thought an experience outside the Jesuit fold would be helpful later.

JESUIT SOLIDARITY

Jesuits have a tradition of helping each other, especially if another Jesuit is in need. So when the instalment for the first quarter tuition from MISEREOR was late, a fellow Jesuit from my Province, Fr Emil D'Cruz, put down $2,000 (it would be about five times as much today) to save my admission. To get to the University of Chicago meant an hour commuting, including two ten-minute walks on either side of the 'L', as the mass transit system is called in the 'Windy City'. In autumn, these walks were unpleasant but in December, when the chill factor was below freezing, they were close to unbearable. I no longer felt cold, only the numbing pain. However, I was saved from hypothermia by another Jesuit friend who gave me his old car. It probably had no resale value but had a year's insurance worth over $600 on it! These were lessons in how we Jesuits share our monies and goods: *Societas Jesu, societas amoris* (The Society of Jesus is a Society of love).

LATE-NIGHT TRUNK CALL

That summer while I was in the midst of preparing for gruelling comprehensive exams to qualify as a doctoral candidate, I missed a late-night trunk call from Bombay. When I was told that my family had called and said they would call again soon, I knew it wouldn't be good news, for my father had long been a cardiac patient. When the call came through, my mother was in tears on the phone. And we didn't have to say much. Though I had many offers of a ticket home from family and friends for my dad's funeral, we decided I'd stay on and keep in touch with my youngest sister, Selena, who was an undergrad in Connecticut, almost as many worlds away as Chicago was from Bombay.

I was alone in Chicago when my dad passed away on 9 April 1975. It was one of the hardest experiences for me that year. Providentially, Fr Macia, who was with me at St Xavier's, was in Chicago, on a brief study break at Loyola University, and he generously spent time with me. He knew my family and we just talked about old times and faraway places. Likewise, Fr Packy (Francis) MacFarland too kept me connected with my folks, writing long weekly letters on 'aerogrammes'. Nothing really fills the emptiness left behind by the passing away of a loved one, but being with people who knew the person you loved helps greatly to recall happier memories, though the healing itself takes years.

My sister, Selena, who was studying at Fairfield University in Connecticut, was being given a hard time by the campus security where she worked. They kept posting her on the late-night watch at the periphery of the campus in winter on open ground. Young women are never given such dangerous appointments after dark. With my encouragement, she threatened to charge them with gender and ethnic discrimination. It worked and she was instantly re-assigned to the Central Communications Security Office, indoors. Selena visited Chicago and later that year she came again with Mum.

All this helped me come to terms with the loss, and the healing was beginning but we'd just have to let it take its time. I know that if I loved my dad less, my sense of loss would be less too, yet I couldn't deny my love in spite of the emptiness his absence brought now; or rather I could affirm it precisely because of his loss.

I invited both my mother and sister to visit me in Chicago before they went on to Canada to spend the summer with their relatives and friends. The hospitality of the parishioners in Chicago, where I was in residence, particularly that of Bonnie and Jack Hickey and my friends at the university from my study group, especially Silvia Pedrasa, Charles Chapelle and a few others, really helped us heal.

Yet for many months I felt this sea of sadness flooding my heart, especially when there was no one to share it with. This then is the price we pay for love lost: we pay it in the coin of pain and grief. But would I have wanted to love him less to ease my ache now? I wrote about it later:

Unfinished Farewells

He never gave himself the time to age
and I cannot ever imagine him old.
He was so active, always on the go
getting the job done,
moving on to the next.
His goodbyes were always
brief and to the point
somewhat hurried, sometimes half-done.
Not for him the lingering
'bye-byes' of our clan,
the 'dear Octopus' that hugged us
in its unfailing grasp,
as we, reluctant to let go,
longing to hang on,
made hesitant efforts
to disengage, our interwoven lives
of endless memories
and family lore.

His final farewell,
improvised and unexpected,
over even before it ever began,
left so much 'unfinished business'
that might have filled
this eventide of

sunsets by the sea.
If only it could be
just possible for him to see
how he could ease his pace,
give himself the room
to rest his heart
at home with treasured memories.

But now he's home at last,
the memories are ours
to share and care and carry on.

When I said goodbye at Santa Cruz
it was not the first time
I was going away,
though for how long this time
I couldn't say.

I wondered when
we'd meet again,
would he visit where I was going
or have to wait
till I came home again?

Airport waiting is a practiced art.
Never his forte, that's for sure.
But now it was a welcome start
to unhurried farewells
this time at last,
as we talked the half night through
until my flight was due.

Nothing's further than a call today,
I said up front, half convinced myself,
not quite realizing how

far away are some places,
beyond all telephonic spaces,
where neither of us as yet
had thought to go.

So when that dreaded call came through
that fateful Friday night, I was many galaxies away,
cut off from him by sound and sight.

No phone could reach him then
too late I realized
the unhurried farewell
at that airport night
had been our last goodbye.

His trust still gives me courage
and sends me on my way
daring me to dream
new worlds still far away.

His optimism lights my hope
against a hopeless world,
it stills my restless waiting in
my sometimes senseless world.

His teasing humour
still makes me laugh
with him and at myself.
From his large heartedness
I've learnt to stretch
my every means
and reach beyond my grasp.
From him I learn
how not to panic
in a crisis

hold the tiller firm
set my sail against the wind
remain uncompromised
in honesty and faith
even when betrayed by
unfair plays and hidden deals
that take advantage of one's trust.
From cruel misfortunes
he protected us
his joie de vivre
infected us
and saw us through
the dark unto the dawn
as long as he stood guard.

My knees still knock
When I hear the fire truck go by,
remembering how once
the flames engulfed
my childhood home,
took my world and
everything we had
into the chill December night;
but for his decisive presence
we escaped with just our lives.

But looking back was not for him.
Picking up the pieces
of our charred, scared lives
he put together for us all
another future
new hopes, new dreams,
a newer, braver world.

When with all the weight
of my nineteen years
I solemnly declared:
'I'm leaving home
for Vinayalaya.
I'm joining the Jesuits,
I won't be coming back.'
To my mother this was like
a death in the family.
But he reassured her
'The boy's not serious, he's a clown.'
But to me he said:
'Be a good one if you must,
no half-measures
will ever please
yourself or me,
do not betray my trust.'

'It matters less what others say
if you can stay the course,
your achievement will outlast success
the inner spirit must come first.'

And so his ceaseless quest
to do his best
inspires in me
a restlessness
that haunts me so,
I cannot settle for
a comfort zone,
when just beyond
the horizon, impossible
dreams become possible,
if only one would stretch enough
to reach the lowering sky,

If only I had told him then
how proud I was of him,
my father and my friend.
Too late now, I hope
He hears me yet and smiles.

(22 September 2003)

Over the years as more of my near and dear ones cross the bar, my comprehension of grief and the sense of loss it brings has matured, and I have been able to write about the void it leaves:

Grief

Grief cannot be shared,
for it is mine alone.
Grief is a dying within me,
a great emptiness, a frightening void.
It is loneliness,
a sickening sorrow at night,
a terrible dread on waking.

Another's words do not help.
A reasoned argument explains little
for having tried too much.
Silence perhaps is the best response.
Not the silence that is a pause in speech,
awkward and unwanted,
but one that unites heart to heart.

Love, speaking in silence, is the way into
the void of another's grief.
The best of all, loves comes silently,
and slowly, to soften the pain,
and begin to dispel the lowering darkness.

It is the love of God, warm and true,
which will touch the grieving heart and heal it.
He looks at the grieving person and has pity,
for grief is a great aching pain.
He came among us to learn about our grief
and much else too, this Man of sorrows.
He knows. He understands.
I pray that grief will yield to peace—in time.

(February 2013)

PEER STIMULATION

What was a great help in preparing for the comprehensive exams was the study group we put together with a few older students from our cohort; two conscientious objectors to the draft, one ex-marine, one faculty wife, and a Cuban divorcée. We would divide the sections of the reading list between us and make presentations to the others. There was no syllabus, just pages and pages of required and recommended reading. Such group study was a lively way of getting some depth in our understanding of the topics and enjoying the interaction as well. Indeed, I learned more with my cohort than from my teachers. I believe this peer stimulation is one the most valuable experience of graduate learning.

Long after we all dispersed from Chicago, some of us still are in touch and exchange notes on where we are at and how it is going. I have visited Sylvia Pedraza in Ann Arbor, Michigan, where she is now a professor. We recall Chicago with much nostalgia.

DISSERTATION PROPOSAL

After completing my course work in 1976, I began work on my dissertation project proposal racing to finish, keeping in mind the sane advice I got in Toronto: 'A good dissertation is a finished dissertation. If it's not finished, it's not a dissertation in the first place.' This was the crucial test: if you had to be stopped because you were just not good enough, this is when your doctoral committee did it. But once this hurdle was crossed, the rest was usually a cruise to the finish.

I decided I'd work on college education in Bombay University. But first, I had to put a dissertation proposal together. One of the professors on my committee, Dr Charles Bidwell, a specialist in education, was a very correct, bow-tied professorial type. When I asked him to be on my committee, I tried to impress him with the policy implications of the topic; he cut me short with: 'Young man, if there are no theoretical considerations, I'm not interested.'

Another, Dr Philip Foster, an expert on Africa, moderated my enthusiasm for policy recommendation with: 'Just because there are problems in the world, don't imagine they can all be solved!'

The third, Dr Terry Clark, was into urban studies and aggregated data collection and analysis. I asked him to chair the committee and he accepted. But first I had to work on a dissertation proposal to meet the intellectual demands of the University of Chicago.

PROFESSIONAL PREJUDICE

The proposal was on arts and science colleges in Bombay University. My fieldwork was to be in the city. I thought this would initiate me into my later work in the college. As a cautionary measure I sent the proposal draft to some senior Jesuits at St Xavier's college for their feedback. I thought, if I was to work with them, I might as well start right away.

I was taken aback by the strong negative feedback I got from one senior Jesuit there. He thought it was not professional enough, 'We professionals know better than this!' But he changed his mind once the committee approved my proposal. However, there was little difference between the proposal he saw and the one I submitted later except for a suggested case study that eventually was dropped as superfluous. I asked but he never explained to me the difference between the two he seemed to have earlier found.

Another, Fr Macia, who wanted to focus on Jesuit colleges on a similar trope, was happy to work together as a team and I would honestly have loved to work with him. But our paces and methodologies, foci and orientations were quite different: I was in a hurry; he wasn't. My methodology was more quantitative, his more qualitative; my focus more secular, his more religious; my orientation more theoretical insight, his more historical context. I was halfway through my proposal, he had still to begin. I was young and brash, he was older and more sober. However, I still regret the missed opportunity.

CENTRED PERIPHERY

My dissertation proposal was entitled: *Structure and Performance: An Organizational Analysis of Arts and Science Colleges in Bombay University*. All went well until the mandatory final hearing open to the rest of the department. Only the chair was there for this hearing, the other committee members had passed the proposal in absentia treating the hearing as a formality since I had been working with them from the start. But then an old Indophile, who was an emeritus at the 'centre' that left others at the 'periphery', showed up for my proposal hearing unannounced. He was not pleased at being left out of the committee. I tried to explain he was on sabbatical out of the country when the committee was formed, but he would have none of it. How could a new arrival on the 'periphery' leave out a veteran at the 'centre'? He grilled me for three quarters of an hour and more and kept me waiting for another three quarters, which were the longest in my life. I thought I was going down and would have to start over again. He crossed me in the corridor with a gruff, 'Good evening,' as he was leaving, 'Mr Clark will speak to you.'

However, when I came into his office Mr Clark was smiling. The old professor emeritus wanted me to use a qualitative methodology and I had chosen a quantitative one. My committee chair suggested I make a reconciliatory gesture. So I came up with an open-ended questionnaire for a case study. This satisfied the old man.

So after two years in Chicago, mostly in the Joseph Regenstein Library—I used to call it 'Life with Joseph'—I was on my way to the Montreal Olympics of 1976 at the invitation of Munawar, my old school friend who still lived in Toronto at the time. There, Nadia Comaneci, the perfect 'ten' gymnast—just fourteen at the time—stole our hearts.

RESEARCH DESIGN AND FIELDWORK

My field survey design called for an hour's closed-ended interview with a sample of some 440 teachers from twenty-two colleges, spread through 280 departments, where the senior-most and junior-most in each department were interviewed. I did 327 interviews myself; my old students did the rest. Finally, there were twenty-one open-ended interviews about an hour and a half long on an average. These were dispersed across a wide spectrum of persons with different perspectives and interests, from college principals and administrators as representatives of the managements to union leaders and activists in the field.

The Emergency of 1975 had been lifted in 1977 and an election called. The Janata Party as a united opposition was hurriedly patched together with ten-rupee donations from common people. When the results were announced late at night, people tumbled into the streets bursting with joy: 'Indira Gandhi haar gayi, Indira Gandhi haar gayi' (Indira Gandhi has lost, Indira Gandhi has lost). However, the Janata Party's Gandhian socialism, to which even the present-day BJP (Bharatiya Janata Party) then subscribed, lasted only as long as Jayaprakash Narayan, its charismatic leader, did. In the aftermath of his demise, it began to unravel in the scramble for power and position. (Will Gandhian socialism, the party's official ideology, ever make a comeback now with the present religious nationalism sweeping the hustings?)

While these momentous events were going on, I was going from college to college to interview teachers. The sample included all the city arts and science colleges except for the one all-women's college at the time. I was told by the vice-principal there that the college had already done their own study. The principal said the exact opposite: that they were planning to do one of their own. I guessed they didn't trust an outsider to do it for them. A pity, I thought, because this women's college would have provided an interesting point of comparison to the other co-ed colleges in the sample.

All the other affiliated arts and science colleges in the Bombay City limits did join in the study, though the cooperation from the faculty members being interviewed varied. One head of department, after long explanations sought from me, nonchalantly refused to be interviewed. But there were also breakthrough moments. One of the academics made and broke three consecutive appointments with a student-interviewer,

Danny Rebello. Finally, Danny told him that he was irresponsible and a set a bad example for students; the professor was shamed into giving the interview.

I found the one reason that got these professors on board was not the recommendations I came with, not the prestige of the University of Chicago, not the importance of the project, but the rather down-to-earth plea: 'I am trying to do my doctorate; can you help me?'

'Oh, then of course!' Personalized appeals do still count here.

I returned to Chicago a year and a half later in January 1978 after coding and card-punching in the data on computer cards. This had to be done by hand and then the material had to be fed in batches into the mainframe computer at the Tata Institute of Fundamental Research (TIFR) and checked again at the University of Chicago computer centre. This was the process followed before the arrival of the personal computers with their immediate feedback on the screen. The analysis had to be done and after that the writing up of the dissertation could happen.

I returned to Chicago for a second stint to write up my dissertation. This time I was a resident priest in another working-class parish at the edge of the Hispanic ghetto, St Francis Xavier Parish, in Avondale. Most of my days were spent in my room hammering out my dissertation on an electric typewriter, which a kindly assistant parish priest, Fr David Gallegos, lent me. I visited the university to use the library and the mainframe computer in the centre there. The parishioners were bemused at how much time I spent in my room. One of the more forward ones asked, 'What do you do such long hours in your room?' I said, 'I'm writing a dissertation.'

'What's that?'

'It's like writing a book,' I ventured.

After a few weeks he inquired again, 'How's it going, Father? How many pages have you written?' I was struggling to put the data together and get a proper perspective on it, so I truthfully replied that I had just done only a few pages.

'You're not working very hard then, are you now, Father?' Nothing like a good reality check from a down-to-earth layperson.

Here I was struggling with processing my data on a mainframe at the university. This meant you lined up for your computing job and any error in the punch cards of the programme would mean the job would be rejected. This sent you back to find the error, do the corrections and join the end of the line to get your job processed again! For an amateur like me, it was really frustrating. I would sometimes be in the computer centre in the basement twelve straight hours, except for short survival breaks. And this guy thought I wasn't working enough!

CONCLUDING IN A DREAM

Eventually, after several months of toiling and struggling, hobbling and bubbling, the problematique was posed and the perspective focused, the historical background sorted out, the data analyzed and written up and conclusions drawn out. However, a final summing-up seemed to elude me. What did all this add up to? I needed a concluding chapter where all the loose ends were brought together and tied up. But I was stuck with writer's block.

Then one sleepless-restless night at 2.00 a.m., it all came together in my head like a pattern in the firmament as in a dream. I was startled wide awake. I got up and actually wrote down the main points by hand, since I didn't want the clatter of the typewriter to wake the parish house up, elaborated them a bit in a couple of pages so as to not lose the significant nuances, and then I went back to sleep. I slept well for I knew I had the outline of the concluding chapter. From then on it was an easy ride home.

JOINING THE GUILD

It was just a couple of months before my dissertation was finalized and approved by my committee and went up for defence before the department. The custom was to invite a professor from outside the department to sit in on the defence. The senior professor from politics whom I approached declined since he was not on my committee. But again, he was on sabbatical in India and I didn't want an absentee committee member. In fact, if he was on the committee he couldn't have been an outside invitee! This had my own head of department somewhat nonplussed but he asked me not to make an issue of it. Eventually, the professor who had taught me my first course and was now in law school, Dr Edward Laumann, agreed to sit in on my defence.

The dissertation defence at the University of Chicago is more a celebration than a grilling. The candidate is given a chance to present what he knows, not probed for what he doesn't. The defence began at 2.00 p.m. It was an open invitation and some of my friends had turned up on the day to give me moral support as it were. When it was over, close to 4.00 p.m, the committee members came over to congratulate me.

One of the professors whom I had first approached had always been very formal. He would greet me as 'Mr Heredia', the customary greeting at the university. As he got to know me better, I became Fr Heredia, then Rudolf, and finally at the end of my defence he came up to me with a warm handshake and said, 'Congratulations, Rudi! This is one of the best defences I've sat on.' I knew now I finally belonged to the guild.

After the defence, we went into a departmental lounge for a sherry hour that lingered on for a bit. Then a close friend from our study group, Charles Chappelle, took me over to his place saying: 'Rudi, I may never finish my own PhD, but goddamnit, I will celebrate yours.' We knocked back a couple of beers before going out to dinner with our old study group. It was way past midnight when they dropped me off at the parish and the priests of the parish were waiting with a bottle of Jim Beam for another round of cheers. No one had turned into a pumpkin as yet, and we cheered on into the early hours of the morning.

It must have been past 3.00 a.m. when we broke up. I dragged myself out of bed for the 7.00 a.m. Mass in the Church and after service, I called my friend's place to find out if he had got home safe. A weary voice replied: 'What did you guys get up to? What did you do to my husband?' So he was safe in bed, with a bad hangover perhaps, and I went back to mine. 'All's well that ends well.'

WINGING HOME

On my way back, I visited my family in Tokyo: my sister Chantal Pinto and her husband Francis with their two little imps, Dev and Vivan, five and six years old, whom my mother was helping to babysit. Compared to Japanese children who are so well behaved and always indulged, these two gremlins were all over the place, bringing it down.

What a wondrous, strange and beautiful land this is, which once had terrible destruction wreaked upon it. I recall standing at ground-zero at Hiroshima and looking around at the horrendous destruction preserved as a war memorial. It all happened in a silent flash of light followed by a deadly roll of thunder. I felt a chill going down my spine. The peaceful beauty of a Zen temple or monastery was a real enigma in contrast to this.

My time at the University of Chicago gave me an intellectual rigour and confidence, I hope not arrogance. For these, I'm forever grateful, not just to the professors there, but also to my colleagues, and the larger University community. The study-group that a few of us who were older than the rest of our cohort had put together had help personalize the university experience and it lasted long after we finished there, and went on our separate journeys.

JESUIT FINISHING SCHOOL

I returned to India in mid-1979 for my tertianship in Dindigul, Tamil Nadu, the last year of Jesuit formation. South India was a new part of the country for me. It has a long and rich history with the Church and the Society. With Fr Tony Coelho as our tertian master, those six months in Dindigul were a wonderful experience. This was quite different from the novitiate and was meant to be a kind of Jesuit finishing school, after which young Jesuits are ready for the world: completely committed, and totally detached, men of God and men in the world, together as companions on mission, bonded as friends in the Lord, men for whom the greater good they seek lies ahead, not behind.

RESTLESS JESUIT

This creates a certain restlessness and must be combined with a restfulness, a coincidence of opposites, which is the true sign of an authentic mystic. This is the Jesuit 'magis', the challenge in the Ignatian Spiritual Exercises always to discern the 'more excellent offering', the more universal good. For, as St Ignatius taught, 'the more universal the good, the more divine'. If a Jesuit settles into a comfort zone, he is dead already as a son of Ignatius, only he has forgotten to lie down—as my mother would say of some people!

A co-novice of mine who left the Society a decade after joining, just before doing his theology, had settled down into a happy marriage. While studying in Chicago, I visited him at was his home in Milwaukee. That day it was his turn for house-sitting and he was feeding his baby girl her lunch. He was really a good father. I told his wife: 'You have tamed the beast.'

'Not really, he still needs his Jesuit friends,' she replied.

'But he has you now,' I countered.

She ruefully answered, that wasn't enough, 'He still has that Jesuit restlessness in him!'

For myself I can say I don't have a sense of closure until I'm over the tipping point of what I'm working on. And then I'm not at ease until I have my teeth into a new project. This can become an unhealthy situation, unless I can find the time to ease my pace and rest my heart. For this we must have an existential realization that we must work committedly as if it all depends on us, and pray earnestly because it all depends on God. But the opposite is equally true: work detachedly because it all depends on God, and pray earnestly as if it all depended your prayer. But I'm still less than halfway there in this mystical coincidence of opposites.

SCHOOLMEN'S OPTION

On returning to the Bombay province in 1979, I had six months before the academic year began at Xavier's. I was asked to do a survey of our schools. This was a delicate and sensitive issue with our schoolmen, who were very much on the defensive after the 32nd General Congregation in its Decree 4 called Jesuits to the service of faith and the promotion of justice as our mission. Our elite schools seemed to be out of sync with this option for the poor, given the constituency they served. This was unfortunate and short sighted. We needed to reorient all our institutions to this new mission and there were surely many creative ways of doing this with our vast and diverse network of schools and colleges.

At a schoolmen's meeting of our province, all agreed, even if somewhat apprehensively, to participate in the study of our schools, which I was commissioned by the Provincial to conduct. For them it was like taking a leap of faith and I was asked to make a statement of my faith: 'Do you believe that our schools are doing good work?' one of them solemnly intoned. It was like the administering of an oath of office or rather of allegiance!

However, I misjudged the situation then. Like a good, newly minted professional researcher, I answered: 'But isn't that what the study is to find out?' My answer was honest but not diplomatic. Unfortunately, they all felt threatened, perhaps too settled in their comfort zones or already haunted by their own doubts. A gloomy sullen silence settled on the group and the meeting ended on that unfortunate note. What the schoolmen wanted was a reassurance from me, what they got was a statement of critical intent.

I was all set to begin the study, when a few days later the Provincial called me and asked if I would mind if the study was scrapped. It seemed some schoolmen had called in to oppose the study, and the Provincial felt he had to give in. The alternative of making the schoolmen take responsibility and opt out of the study, or at least opt in was not considered.

I feel the Provincial's decision did save the schoolmen from the responsibility of choice. Perhaps he just had to stay the survey at that difficult time. However, I don't believe there has been a serious critical profession study of our schools since, only self-evaluations that have turned out to be awkwardly self-laudatory, hardly credible beyond the schoolmen and their schools' own beneficiaries. The schoolmen seemed too traumatized by the 32nd General Congregation's Decree 4, which demanded that all our works exercise an option for the poor in 'the service of faith and the promotion of justice'. This meant finding creative ways of being both excellent academically and relevant for the poor as well.

Nine years later, in 1989, at the Central American University in El Salvador, six Jesuits were brutally martyred for standing up to the injustice and violence of the national regime. They showed us all how our educational institutions can be witnesses for justice and stand with the poor and be both intellectually excellent and socially relevant.

Fr John Macia's doctoral dissertation on *Organizational Purpose and Distinctive Character of Colleges: A Study of Jesuit Colleges in India* (1982) for the Tata Institute of Social Sciences on three of the oldest Jesuit university colleges in India—St Joseph's, Trichinopoly; St Xavier's, Calcutta; and St Xavier's, Bombay—did underscore the same dilemma of excellence and relevence but did not address it. His monumental opus is still lying unpublished and unpolished, as with so many excellent doctoral dissertations by Jesuits. It would seem these degrees are mere qualifications for a job, a position, a status, not part of an on-going learning process in a continuing pedagogic endeavour.

The challenge that the 32nd General Congregation posed to the whole Society of Jesus with its Decree 4, precipitated a crisis for the whole Society in 1976, from which we are emerging more than half a century later. I believe we are still not out of the woods and just might lose nerve and retreat into the shadows. I believe we have lacked the collective imagination and will to contextualize for our day this 'option for the poor', in the new articulation of our mission 'the service of faith and the promotion of justice'.

At times I find myself humming Simon and Garfunkel's 'Sounds of Silence': 'Hello Darkness my old friend, I've come to talk to you again...' We mustn't renege on the legacy of Fr Pedro Arrupe or the Ignatian 'magis' and fail to read and respond to this prophetic silence of the anawim, as the poor are named in the Gospels.

TEACHING AS A VOCATION

When I began teaching at St Xavier's College, I was quite lucky because there was no full-time official teaching position available for me, though my return was known at least a year in advance. The sociology department had its full load so I got a part-time teaching position by scraping together a few required 'Foundation Courses' from other departments that were slightly overburdened. But part-time teaching gave me a great opportunity to do other things as well. Fr Lancelot Pereira, who was the principal and a daring and innovative educationist, urged me to form a Social Science Centre (SSC) to do Social Science Research and invest my surplus energies in it. And so I did in 1980, for I felt part-time teaching alone was not going to be enough to absorb my energy and enthusiasm.

But there were some reality checks that brought me down to earth.

Once after I had given what I thought was a motivating and inspiring lecture to a class of eighty students that left me feeling exhausted and worn, two bright young things came up to me to say: 'We feel so sorry for you.' I wondered why. Their answer was a revelation for me: 'You try so hard, but you don't realize we aren't that interested!' How do I motivate these students to want to do more, to reach beyond their grasp? 'Encouraging to fly' was the college motto and here I fell flattened on the ground!

On another memorable occasion a young person was so annoyed at my single-minded focus on the task and my seeming disinterest in the person, that she stormed out of my office and on the way out picked up some books off my table and threw them out of the window. I was so nonplussed, I didn't know how to respond so I quietly went into the garden, picked up the books lest they get dumped into the dustbin, came back and waited for an apology. All I got the next day was a limp, 'But I'm only seventeen.'

This left me even more befuddled until I recognized this might well be a temperamental person's way of apologizing. I knew I too could throw a counter tantrum. But then I recalled the counsel of a wise old Jesuit mentor: 'Never be harsh on people; there are many mysteries hidden in each one of us.'

SOCIAL SCIENCE CENTRE

Fr Alfred de Souza, the Director of the Indian Social Institute (ISI) Delhi, truly a gentleman and a scholar, had urged me to join his team at ISI. He thought I'd fit in there better. Perhaps he was right. However, I preferred combining teaching with research at St Xavier's College, as being closer to the ground reality. Delhi, I've always felt was very far from India! I started the Social Science Centre (SSC) in 1980 almost immediately on joining St Xavier's thanks to the generous moral support from some farsighted older Jesuits in the community.

Jesuits in St Xavier's once had a strong intellectual presence on the national stage: Fr Henry Heras (1888–1955), the historian, an expert on the Mohenjo-Daro and the Harrapan civilization; Fr Alolf Esteller (1888–1955) the Sanskritist, who studied the Rigveda for fifty years, trying to apply modern literary criticism to the text; Fr Hermenegild Santapau (1903–70) the botanist and Director of the Botanical Survey of India; Fr Ferdinand Caius (1877–1944) who worked on the medicinal plants of India. But I strongly felt there should be a balance between the 'field and the desk': the experience in the field had to be articulated at the desk and the ideas from the 'texts' needed to be verified on the 'ground', even as the process is mentored by the teacher in the class and facilitated by the activist in the field.

HOLISTIC PEDAGOGY

I wanted to add an out-reach to our teaching and a reflective dimension to our field involvement. This meant an action-reflection praxis which activists never quite understood and intellectuals didn't really appreciate. Teachers felt it was poor pedagogy, and administrators found it was too messy to standardize and fit into the old evaluation mould.

In the beginning it was hard going on all sides for me: work-week teaching in the classroom, weekend fieldwork in the district and in between learning from the students in the cafeteria. But then it made a lasting impression on me, for as I mentioned before, I have always felt I've learnt more than I've taught my students.

I found that the students, the young ones, responded the best to this holistic pedagogy. Many told me that they found it exhilarating. It was a growth opportunity for some younger teachers too, though no doubt, there were some growing pains as well. The older teachers, set in their ways and comfortable perhaps in the power structures, could find it intimidating; and the diffident ones found it terrifying. Not everyone was willing to leave their comfort zone of the classroom to experiment in a strange new land in the field. Eventually however, some got the point of being organic intellectuals and not just ad-hoc activists or abstract theoreticians, or rote pedagogues, whichever is worst.

PARTICIPATORY ACTION–RESEARCH

The Social Science Centre was to focus upon participatory action-research on issues of social concern. It was meant to add a reflection-dimension to our action-projects in the field. This involved looking at questions and issues in the field, and seeking answers and responses from a competent professional resource. The methodology entailed the following steps not necessarily in the same sequence: the centre undertook to provide the professional competence for the research design, monitoring the data collection and its analysis; the NGO partner provided the fieldworkers for the collection and tabulation of the data; a joint discussion of the findings and learnings; a commitment by the partner in the field to implement and carry forward what was feasible; and finally a report to be published in the public domain.

The students of St Xavier's were used to social service camps in which they offered shramdaan, the gift of their manual labour. This was to be different. Now the students would be asked to offer the gift of their knowledge, budhidaan, but they would also receive in exchange new invaluable, experiential insights and be enriched in the process. This was to be a live-in, a study-camp, 'teach-in' or rather a 'learn-in'.

Moreover, where feasible, I taught and encouraged students to do a practicum to test their ideas on the ground. This is what they enjoyed most; I could see that in the endless discussions and arguments that were generated. I would sit in but as far as possible leave the conclusions open-ended, holding them accountable only to fact and reason. There would be no 'by-hearting', memorizing, as is customary here.

When on 18 January 1982, about 250,000 mill workers of Mumbai struck work, it was the beginning of an epic strike, one that has not been officially called off yet. A small group of students decided to study the strike extensively as part of the fieldwork for a course I was teaching. I supported them in the idea. They spent time at the mill gates where they would meet mill workers and talk to them about the issues involved. They also met union officials and even the supremo, Dr Datta Samant, himself. I can hardly think of a more effective way of sensitizing students to the labouring classes—as long as the teacher moderates the process and other external inputs are provided.

RELEVANCE AND EXCELLENCE

I found most students were more concerned with doing well in examinations than in gaining some mastery over the subjects they had chosen to study. I wanted them to realize that mastering the subject meant more than good examination performance. A qualification does not mean competence, at least not in our system, where the relationship between the two is sometimes quite arbitrary.

And yet, too often, academic excellence of an institution is measured by examination performance, by the marks students get in their public exams, which is valued over social relevance as reflected in its contribution to individual and structural change. The greater common good is hardly a serious consideration at all. Being men and women for others too can easily become an afterthought rather than a planned and integrated agenda.

Now and then an ex student would meet me on neutral ground and say: 'I was your student.' I remember one of these encounters.

'I was your student,' said the young woman.

'Really, was it a good experience?' I asked, my usual response.

She began to give the ambiguous Indian head wiggle and then after a pause she decided to opt for honesty: 'You spoilt my life, you taught me things I couldn't practise.'

I asked, 'Would you have wished it otherwise?'

The answer was abrupt and conclusive: 'No!'

ISSUES OF SOCIAL CONCERN

The first of these participatory researches began in 1980 and ran for two years; the follow-up, two more. Later in 1992, it was published as *Tribal Education for Community Development: A Study of Schooling in the Talasari Mission Area* (Concept Publications. New

Delhi, 1992). This was an extensive study of some of the earliest primary schools begun by the mission in the area. What emerged was how schools and the parish supported each other, though the weightage once given to the parish was changing in favour of the school. The second was on the Maharashtra Prabhodan Seva Mandal (MPSM) later published as *Voluntary Action and Development: Towards a Praxis for Non-Government Agencies* (Concept Publications. New Delhi, 1988). This was a model farmers' NGO, attempting to capitalize on government schemes and put together a more effective model of development.

The third, published during the pavement dwellers, agitation, *Settlements and Shelter: Alternative Housing for the Urban Poor in Bombay* (Committee for the Right to Housing. Bombay, 1985; also published by ISI, New Delhi, in their Monograph Series No. 26, 1986) is self-explanatory. This was followed up with *Urban Housing and Voluntary Agencies: Case Studies in Bombay* (Institute of Social Sciences. New Delhi, 1989).

The Social Science Centre had been accompanying the Jesuit mission in Raigad district since 1989 as part of its commitment to bring the reflection-dimension to our field-action. In 1992, a formal trust—the Janhit Vikas—was set up and the Centre began a participatory survey of the Kathkaris. The Kathkaris were a small marginalized tribe the Jesuit NGO was working with in the twelve centres they had opened in the district with the help of religious sisters of different congregations. The field work was completed in 1994, before I left to join ISI Delhi, and was written and published from there as *Tribal Identity and Minority Status: The Kathkari Nomads in Transition* (with Rahul Srivastava) (Concept Publications. New Delhi, 1994).

FORMATION REVIEW COMMISSION

In 1987, I had asked my Provincial to allow me research as my first priority. This was taken up by the POI (Provincial of India) as he was then called; later he was referred to as the Provincial of South Asia (POSA), and now President, Jesuit Conference of South Asia (JCSA). But what's in a name, a rose by any other name will smell the same. But so far Provincials have not been mistaken for roses! The POI in 1987 asked that I be released for the Indian Social Institute, Delhi (ISI-D), but the principal of St Xavier's, who was short of Jesuit staff, objected and even wrote to the Fr General to stymie the request.

Some years, later I was pulled out of college anyway to chair the Formation Review Commission (FRC) from 1990 to 1992. This committee was tasked with reviewing and renewing the training of young scholastics in South Asia. After the changes brought in by Vatican II and our 32nd General Congregation in its Decree 4, the formation of our scholastics had to be oriented to our redefined mission.

The Commission was a team of four Jesuits of diverse backgrounds and varied experiences: Fr Michael

Raj, ex-Provincial of Madurai Province; Fr T.K. John, professor of Vidyajyoti; Fr Silvanus Kiro assistant to the POI; and I. We divided ourselves into pairs and travelled to the Houses of Formation across the South Asian Assistancy (i.e. a group of Jesuit provinces on the Subcontinent). In the first year, Fr T.K. John traversed some 50,000 kms by train and bus, since the North Zone allotted to him covered the largest area in the South Asian Assistancy; in the West Zone I covered approximately 40,000 kms. The South and Central Zones were more compact and less travelling was needed. After a series of meetings and discussions, spread over two years, we proposed an 'apprenticeship-model', which was elaborated in the final report of the Commission

But to train good apprentices demanded good master craftsmen. And there's the rub. We have too many teachers who 'lecture', who make passive learners of scholastic-seminarians, not enough 'formators' who challenge them to be active participants in the pedagogic process. As the then Provincial of South Asia (POSA) used to say: 'formation is too important to be left to formators alone'.

This was to be formation not just *for* but *in* mission, accompanied and personalized, not an assembly-line production. But the major common houses, the scholasticates of the Assistancy were reluctant and slow to change.

In one house, the FRC team members assigned there were ignored for the first two days of their visit.

Finally on the third and last day, the resident faculty wanted the FRC team to reschedule the review process over again. There was so much resistance, I was not sure it wouldn't spring up again. However, in retrospect, not yielding to this suggestion was a serious mistake on the part of the FRC team. It only upped the ante on their opposition.

COMMON GROUND TO HIGHER GROUND

At one point the whole process seemed to be falling apart. A group of Jesuit formators—about fifty of them—was meeting formally as the Formation Commission for the South Asian Assistancy in Vidyajyoti, our theologate in Delhi, in October 1991. Desperately searching for a way to bring it back on track, I decided we would return to basics. I asked them to pause in silence for a full five minutes and then share in a few sentences the 'myth' each one lived by, i.e., the deepest motivation of their Jesuit lives. After a pregnant silence, which seemed an eternity, all fifty of us sitting in a circle, by turn articulated some version of the Jesus myth we had internalized over the years: one had a Marian tilt, another chose not to share. We had found common ground from which to proceed together to higher ground.

The lesson to be learnt from this experience was that we Jesuits must build on the fundamentals that unite and inspire us; that is our strength. Focusing on the accidentals that may divide and polarize us becomes our weakness. I believe, over the years, our formation and mission are more in sync now. The glass may be half full or half empty, that matters little. The point is that the Jesuit 'magis' demands we strive to fill it.

The FRC experience confirmed for me that teamwork was *the* asceticism for our day, a dying of the self (self-will, self-love, self-interest) so that one might work together with others as team-mates, to become companions on a mission, friends in the Lord. Our complex world requires a corporate or collectively organized response. The sooner we learn to work together as a team, the more effective will we be. Not just 'community as mission' as the 35th General Congregation articulated, but 'mission as community' too. For not only does a Jesuit community have a collective mission, but a Jesuit mission must be located in a community which then takes responsibility for it. The implication for our formation then is this: not just formation *for* mission but formation *in* mission too, learning on the job or what has also been called 'service-learning'.

The overall impact of the FRC, I believe, was to bring formation (training) and mission (apostolate) closer, make in-house learning and out-reach experience more integrated, make intra-mural living and extra-mural residence more compatible. However, its greatest impact was on the formation houses of the provinces, the novitiates and juniorates. The complex structures of the national institutions, philosophates and theologates made change difficult. Three decades later, though we are still far ahead from where we were in 1990, we are still not where we'd like, and ought, to be: formation in phases, moving from one to the next only when the goals of the previous phase are satisfactorily attained, not in stages following each other automatically on a predetermined timeline; more active student-teacher engagement in a dialogue, not a one-way teacher input in the form of a monologue; more personalized student accompaniment, learning in tutorial groups, in outreach service ministries—thus bringing Jesuit formation and Jesuit mission closer together. Moreover, it implied an interplay that had to be subtle, creative, personalized and intense. Or rather, the FRC was suggesting that the formation must be not just *for* but *in* mission too.

MY FIRST AVATAR AT ISI, DELHI

After I finished with the FRC, I asked to be a part-time lecturer at St Xavier's, since I wanted to devote more time to the Social Science Centre. But the principal wanted a full-time person, so when the POI asked again that I be assigned to ISI, I was readily released and happy to go. I went with the promise of only research and no administration. The then director of the ISI, Delhi, Fr Jose Murican, was very welcoming. But a few months before I could take up this new assignment he was appointed Provincial superior elsewhere, leaving both the Institute and the Research Department headless. I was asked to fill in.

I told the Provincial of India that I had asked for and was assured time for research, and before I could even start, he was asking me to be the Director! I pointed out that I would not be able to do any research as the Director of the Institute was a full-time administrative appointment. But he and the existing Director insisted it was God's will. I replied I would write to Fr General to find out if this was so. However, before I could write, finally someone was found to accept the directorship, and I was welcomed as research director. It was a very happy ending for all, only I needed an angiogram in 1993. But if anything is to be blamed for that, then it was the FRC, not the Indian Social Institute, Delhi.

My stint at the ISI began only after the FRC report was submitted in 1990. We had a good and productive time in the ISI Department of Research. Each of the four research scholars was to design a research project within the allotted budget and set timelines collectively. As often as was possible, we would have a 'brown bag' lunch together and discuss our projects. I would give my departmental colleagues a long rope but hold them to the deadlines and goals that they set for themselves. This worked very well and we built a great team, of which I still have fond memories.

After two years, the new Rector at Xavier's asked if I would come back and revive the Social Science Centre which had been quite dead. I felt the Research Department was running and stable and ready to be handed over to someone else. So I accepted because I was assured that I wouldn't have any add-on jobs.

However, my transfer was announced so abruptly by the ISI Director that it came as a shock to my colleagues in the department. They felt betrayed and angry; some were even in tears and wouldn't talk to me. It was katti—break-up. Fortunately, the jinx was broken and we were batti—friends again, before I left. I offered to continue editing *Social Action* from Mumbai if needed and did so for a year. I would come to Delhi the week before the issue was due and finalize it. This made my sudden leaving more gradual and acceptable to people in the department.

THE DNT PROJECT

I was back at St Xavier's in 1994 with no formal teaching assignments for my second stint at the SSC; and again this was a very productive time. We built up a team of seven research assistants based in Pune and worked with Denotified and Nomadic Tribes (DNT), who were once categorized by the British colonial government as 'criminal tribes'. A preliminary field survey showed their literacy rate was abysmal, between 1 and 2 per cent. However, the aim of the project went beyond literacy, we wanted to try and give them a sense of self-worth and dignity, 'to read not just the "words", but to read the "world"'; to be not merely literate but conscientized as well.

When we had conducted a literacy programme for Kathkaris, in Raigad district, then considered a semi-primitive tribe, we had observed that they never heard anything positive about themselves either in the children's school textbooks or in the conversations in the marketplace. So we decided to create a series of short texts, one page in the tribal language, and a translation into the state language, Marathi, on the other side. They were meant to be read and discussed, facilitated by a teacher.

The themes were simple, meant for children and neo-literates; we used their own stories, fables and lives. We set up a classroom for children to come and do their own thing—draw pictures, make charts and write their stories. We exhibited these on the walls. It proved a great catalyst in releasing the boundless creative energies of the children.

We expanded the project to nine more tribes, coming out with a brochure for each. We had a conference in Vadodara and another in Satara and finally a third in Delhi in 2001. Together with about a hundred NGOs working with Denotified Tribes, we managed to lobby the Government of India to set up a commission, which eventually got reservation quotas for these tribals.

THINKING TRUST, SQUABBLING FOR SPACE

Unfortunately, the Rector who had brought me back to St Xavier's from Delhi in 1994, Fr Desmond D'Monte, died in a freak accident on the road to Khandala in the summer of 1998 and I was asked to stand in for him and take up the Rectorship of St Xavier's. This time there really was no one else so I had to pick up the slack. There was a desperate need to end the ad-hocism to which St Xavier's College was so prone. There was an organizational near-sightedness that could not think 'trust' holistically. This expressed itself overtly in a scramble for space on campus, though in reality this was a struggle for power despite pious mouthings to the contrary.

The original college had spawned many smaller institutions that piggybacked on the college until they outgrew their dependence and followed their own growth path in another location off campus, e.g., the St Xavier's Institute of Education relocated at Churchgate, and the Xavier's Technical Institute at Mahim. The Xavier's Institute of Management and Xavier's Institute of Communications did not break away and as they expanded, space became a contested issue. The smaller institutes, like the Heras Institute of Ancient Indian History and Culture and the Social Science Centre, found their niche and functioned within those confines.

A larger vision was not uniting the whole campus anymore, so no holistic planning was possible, only ad-hocism, that postpones but cannot resolve the underlying issues. Structural tensions between institutions build up and good PR between personnel are equivalent to a band-aid approach. I constituted a more representative College Governing Board to coordinate the campus institutes and work towards common goals but there was much resistance from individual institutes, protecting their turf rather than sharing their resources. The board became a place to air grievances rather than build synergies.

When it was found critically dangerous to have a large library of one institute on the first floor because the old wooden structure was already unstable, it was proposed to move it to unused space on the ground floor that had once been used by the campus peons. This was contested by some in the College. The Provincial ordered a space audit which showed there was plenty of space available especially for the college, whose classrooms were unused almost half the day. With a little adjustment in the time schedules, if space was used creatively and shared reasonably, there was more than enough for all—to share and even to spare. The contested space on the ground floor that had been unused for many years was suddenly found to be urgently needed by a wannabe Jesuit principal for plans still unmade. But this was still years away, if at all.

So when the naysayers had no more alibis to plead and the new Provincial's decision went against them, they made me the fall guy for pushing the restructuring as the Rector. One Jesuit on the campus even compared it to appropriating 'adivasi land'! Jesuits in St Xavier's College as adivasis! It requires much clownish humour and wit to see any sense in this analogy coming from someone who was not even assigned to the college.

My term as Rector ended in October 2003. On 13 February 2004, the Provincial had told me that he wanted me to stay on the campus to be an intellectual presence there. But on 8 March of the same year, he called up when I was visiting in Delhi to ask why don't I go on sabbatical for two years to any place I chose, anywhere in the world. I said that I didn't need a sabbatical. 'I have a book contract from Penguin, which I want to complete before I go anyplace else.'

The Jesuits pledge obedience and so I told the Provincial that I would, in obedience, go where I was sent. Then I added, 'But now please tell me what has changed. Just last week you said that you wanted me to be an intellectual presence on the campus and now you are asking me to leave the campus.' He had no answer—and no answers have ever been forthcoming—though he did admit that this was unfair.

Clearly this seems to show a crisis of authority, a serious lack of accountability for superiors. I do believe the Peter Principle had kicked in, i.e. success at a lower level earns promotion to a higher one until one reaches one's level of incompetence! Not for these men the laws of ancient Rome, wherein it was 'not the custom of the Romans to give up any man to destruction, before the accused has met the accusers face to face, and has had opportunity to make his defence concerning the matter laid against him' (Acts 25: 16). Just weak egos but strong egotism! I could have appealed to Father General but I didn't.

'Why do you want to stay in a community that doesn't want you?' the Provincial asked me. This was unanswerable, so I said, 'I will go but give me the reason for this sudden change.' I was told there were 'specific things I had said and done' so even he couldn't support me. I never got anything specific from the Provincial who insisted I talk to the Rector. And when I did, he insisted that there was nothing specific but 'in general, you make people uneasy'.

I shuttled between Provincial and Rector until the latter wrote me a note: 'Why don't you just go and give us the space?' There had been no consultation, no community or college team meeting, no meeting of the Trust Governing Body. A young Jesuit in the community even asked me, 'Why are you leaving? I can't understand.'

I replied, 'I never asked to leave. I was told to go. No point in clinging to a community where no one there will stand up for me. I believe God's vineyard is wide and vast, there are many places I can serve.'

Later I found that just two Jesuits had lobbied with the Provincial to have me transferred out of the college. Perhaps I had just too much self-respect—or was it too much pride?—to cling to a community where I was so obviously not wanted. Was I a thorn in their collective side or a challenge they did not want to face? Was it my problem or theirs? And if it was theirs, should I have been penalized or should they have been challenged?

But what goes around comes around. Soon the two main conspirators were quarrelling over—guess what? Space! Surprise, surprise. In a few years, the chief conspirator had alienated the whole Jesuit team with his behaviour. In response the Provincial called for an independent evaluation. That report was even more negative. But it was shared with the Jesuit community only in parts and only for a very limited time and hastily withdrawn.

Eventually the man had to be terminated only to be flattered with compensatory appointments, hurriedly rushed through by the Provincial without the customary procedure.

THE CENTRE FADES OUT

I had thought to conclude my association of twenty-four years at the Social Science Centre in a celebratory silver jubilee year with a series of seminars and lectures. During the course of these, I was going to introduce the new Director so that he would be in contact with all those who had been associated with the Centre. But the new Director would have none of this.

He was confident he would manage on his own and wanted to start with a clean slate. So he began by changing the centre's name to 'Xavier Institute for Social Research and Action' (XISRA). A name change is meant to indicate something new. However, it's often done for just the opposite reason, a cover-up device used by pretentious leaders and politicians to hide their failures. I am not saying this was happening here. However there was not a single serious refereed monograph produced, nor am I aware of any book published, not even a sponsored one. No sustained projects or campaigns were undertaken. The Centre was slowly dying.

A woman academic friend of mine from Oxbridge asked me: 'How could you just give it all up after twenty-four years and walk away?' Before 1 could attempt a reply she answered her own question: 'Oh, but then you're a sadhu; it can be expected of you.' That was a lesson in commitment and detachment I won't easily forget.

When the Centre was moved to Nashik, it left most of its work behind in Mumbai, and never seems to have caught up with it in its new location. Now the Centre has been absorbed into the Maharashtra Prabodhan Seva Mandal (MPSM). Perhaps the downsizing was required for personnel considerations.

Lately the proactive new Director of the Mandal plans to revive the research centre as part of the Mandal in Nashik, for he sees the critical need of a reflection dimension to our field action. I have been asked to help and have very happily and readily agreed.

But guess what happened to the non-performing Director of the Centre? He got 'promoted' to a national-level assignment. *Promoveatur ut removeatur* (Let him be promoted in order that he may be removed!) More of the Peter Principle?

CAMPION INTERLUDE

Campion School, named after the 16th-century English Jesuit Martyr, St Edmund Campion, had been established in 1943. In 1986, a trust was set up by the Jesuits, with the Bombay Jesuit Provincial and the Bombay Archbishop as patrons, who appointed trustees for a six-year renewable term to the Campion School Trust. These elected a Council of Management (CoM), again for an even shorter time-bound three year term renewable once. The CoM ran the School. Each patron had a representative on the trust. The properties still belonged to the Society of Jesus. In 1998, the Archbishop asked for and was given the sole power of attorney as patron. But by 2003 the school was in a mess, with parents screaming on the street outside the Archbishop's House and insulting the Cardinal Archbishop to his face. And so he hurriedly handed the school back to the Jesuits.

While the St Xavier's College imbroglio was still running its course, the same Provincial who had transferred me, asked if I would be his representative to the Board of Trustees of Campion School. I felt my loyalty to the Society demanded that I accept and do my best. The Provincial had now become the sole patron of the trust. Trustees were appointed and held office at his pleasure. A new trust deed had to be written up and a new Board nominated and had to get going. It was a difficult, delicate and onerous task. There were times I really thought we were going under.

Moreover, I was doing this from ISI, Delhi, where I was now appointed. I would come in for quarterly board meetings and as and when needed. It all hinged on the patron nominating the right people for the Board who would then elect the best persons to the CoM to run the school, electing a chair and secretary and appointing a principal. As the Provincial's representative, my role was only to advise and facilitate the process, making sure the school was true to Ignatian ideals, in keeping with its Jesuit character.

It was a wonderful experiment and it worked. Over the next fourteen years, Campion was turned into one of the best day-schools in the country according to various evaluative agencies. The credit goes to the staff and teachers, parents and students and of course the private tuition classes for those who could afford them.

And so, I was once again truly astounded when I was accused by the Provincial of 'bluffing' them all about the say the Jesuits had in the school. The Provincial, one of his consulters and the ex-Provincial (who had helped draft the new constitution), could not find anything about the patron having the final say on any disagreement with the General Body of the Trust, and the trustees holding office at the patron's pleasure.

I found the relevant clause in the Memorandum of Understanding which served as the trust deed and emailed it to the three, highlighting the relevant sentence in red, asking how they could miss it. In reply I was told by the Provincial that they actually wanted more control. Yet all the policy statements from our Jesuit Curia in Rome were calling for greater participation, not greater control.

I can only surmise what was meant was greater control over student admission and staff appointments. These are critical fountainheads of patronage and power that so easily corrode and corrupt. With the declining numbers in many religious orders, including the Society of Jesus, especially in Bombay province, we seem unable or unwilling to grasp the urgency of sharing our mission with others who are like-minded and similarly motivated persons, responsive to the Jesuit spirituality of the magis, not settling into a comfort zone but striving for the greater good and building a cadre of collaborators to work together as an extended Jesuit family.

Finally, after years of pleading to be replaced as the province's representative on the Board by someone who had a closer experience of high schools, I stepped down and the ex-principal of St Xavier's, who had worked to oust me from the college, took my place. A new era in Campion had begun!

Regrettably, the clock has been turned back with the appointment of a retired Jesuit principal once again. Eventually a replacement for him will have to be found. With our aging members and depleted numbers, if vigorous, collaborative and responsible collaborators are not put in place already now, our institutions will be in terminal decline, as is the case with many religious congrgations that are losing their relevance today. 'The words of the prophet are written on the subway walls and tenement halls', but are we reading the words? Are we rushing into the wrong train and failing to get off at the right stop?

SECOND AVATAR AT ISI

I remember how Fr Joseph Neuner, doyen of theology in India and a Vatican II peritus (expert), was transferred from De Nobili College to a district mission station, because the younger faculty—or at least one or two of them—felt they wouldn't be able to grow under his shadow. This was the ugly result of insecurity among the young. Perhaps they could all learn a lesson from Pope Francis, who when asked about the Pope Emeritus staying on in the Vatican, said: 'It's good to have a grandfather in the house.' Fr Neuner would have been a grandfather for all to learn from. Evidently, I couldn't claim the same grandfatherly status at Xavier's.

So when I left the college community, I had to find another to reside in and work from. I approached ISI Delhi. However, the treasurer there insisted I do something in the Institute to earn my keep. I said, 'I have a book contract from Penguin. I'm asking for a place to work. If Penguin had given ISI the contract, you would have come to me and been paying me.'

But the man insisted I pay my way. He understood money in its least interesting form, as a measure of the world's evaluation. He had no sense of scholarly value, unless it could be monetized, and yet he was in a national intellectual centre of the Society! Only old Fr Paul de la Guérivière, *an emeritus in the community,* supported my request.

As a compromise, I agreed to edit *Social Action*, the journal of the institute, as I had done before. I was given an office in the basement, where I worked my tail off for the next six years to fulfil the book contract with Penguin, because I had something to prove. I hardly saw the sun, which was very unwise. By the third year I had submitted the final manuscript of *Changing Gods: Rethinking Religious Conversion in India* (Penguin, 2007) but I paid the price—I had to undergo a cardiac by-pass surgery in April 2005. There is only so much you can push your 'brother ass', as St Francis Assisi would sometimes refer to his often reluctant body.

I had to make a prior down payment of two lakh rupees before the cardiac by-pass operation. The Provincial of South Asia and the ISI superior said to me: 'Do whatever is needed and don't worry about the money.' I will be forever grateful to both, Frs Hector D'Souza and Tom Kunnunkal, for this.

ADMINISTRATION VERSUS SCHOLARSHIP

The ISI superior, Fr Tom Kunnunkal, a Jesuit I deeply respect, once in 2006 asked me: 'Why don't you make a sacrifice for the Society and take up the directorship of the ISI?'

I replied, 'You're right in asking this, but appointing

a suitable Director of ISI is not a new issue for JCSA of which you as a Provincial were a part of once. But they have outsourced their collective responsibility to the POI. So you are asking me to make up for what the JCSA neglected. Is that fair?'

He was silent, but then I think he was one of the few competent administrators who valued intellectual scholarship. I was again asked by the POSA a couple years later, after finishing my first book for Penguin, *Changing Gods*, to be the Director at ISI. I said I'd consider it for one year. The POSA said it must be at least two.

'And after that what?' I asked.

'You can go back to your province.'

I replied, 'Then I might as well return now.'

So I was given the pink slip.

I gave this letter of termination to Fr Tom my superior at ISI, and said that I would not contest it. He took the letter and got the decision reversed. So I started on my second book while continuing to edit *Social Action*.

After a year, in 2008, I was removed from the editorship and it was given to the new director. So I was no longer contributing to ISI, and I became a resident guest in ISI at my province's expense. Once I finished my second book in 2010, *Taking Sides: Reservation Quotas and Minority Rights in India* (Penguin, 2012), I returned to my province, ending my second avatar in ISI.

APPEAL TO FR GENERAL

Now I was a homeless Jesuit. I had no idea where I would be posted. In an ageing province like ours, with fewer young men joining and many more old ones passing on, your appointment depends on who dies! The new Provincial, who had called me back to the province, assured me that I would be given full-time research. But six months after I returned, he asked me to be superior of the Campion community, to which I was now attached, and the manager of the Institute of Education and the Boys Academy, while keeping me on as his representative on the Campion Board.

I asked, 'What about research?'

'You can do that as well,' he said, rather off-handedly.

I felt I was not being heard by the Provincial or the Provincial designate. So after talking to some Jesuit friends, I decided to write to Father General. Once I had done that, I said a prayer because there is no appeal after that. After a while I got a reassuring email saying I was not to worry.

Finally the decision went in my favour. I was happy but the Provincial wasn't.

He asked me, 'Why did you have write to Father General?'

I replied, 'Are you denying my right as a Jesuit to appeal to Father General?'

'No, no,' he exclaimed, 'I meant that...'

I interrupted with, 'Then what are you saying?'

He did not expect this, so he came back with: 'You could have waited till after the province appointments came out.'

He knew as well as I did that once this had happened, it would have made things even more complicated.

A MOTHER'S CALLING

I was fortunate to be in Mumbai through the following years, for this was when my mother's health was failing. Through those years, after having relocated in Goa leaving her hectic life in Mumbai behind, she managed to keep in touch with a surprising number of people both in Bombay and Goa, where she was living out her final years in gratitude and patience, with good cheer and goodwill for all. She was and will always be a tower of strength and a shining example of aging gracefully. I still hear her calling:

Come Home to Me

(A mother's farewell)

Wherever you are, my son, come back to me
Wherever you are, come home to me
Come back to me wherever you are.

And if you can't, don't explain,
I'll understand.
Be safe, wherever you are,

take care wherever you go,
And remember me though I can't be there.

But when you can
do come back to me
in my dreams at least come back to me.
I wait for you in my dreams.

I'll always remember,
How can I forget?
I always will be waiting,
There's little else I can do.

If I don't see you again, my son,
in my dreams I'll wait for you,
I always do, I'll wait for you.
Come home to me.

(12 February 2013)

In her ninety-fifth year, she wrote her family memoir, *It's Been a Long Day: A Nonagenarian Remembers* (Goa 1556, 2012). I can still see her sitting by the river Mandovi flowing past her villa and out to sea, with lights of Panjim twinkling across the water as we sat, recalling the nostalgia of her long rich past and remembering things far away and long ago and praying:

Newman's Prayer

May He support us all the day long,
Till the shades lengthen and the evening comes,
and the busy world is hushed, and the fever of life
 is over,
and our work is done.
Then in his mercy may he give us a safe lodging,
and holy rest, and peace at the last.

I suppose I imagined that she would be there for us as she had always been. Now the evening high-rise shadows of Bombay are engulfing me, and rarely do I get to see the twinkling lights across the harbour on the beach at Uran where as children we spent some of our happiest days. It remained my dad's weekend get-away from the madding crowds of Bombay. It was a place she had always imagined spending a long happy retirement with him, so close yet so far from the big city across the harbour. Verem Villas, where she lived out her declining years, was the closest she could come to that. But now without her life partner.

She was a presence in the colony and had many and frequent visitors. I still draw strength from her memory for she was the centre of our family lives, the matriarch of our 'clan'. I wrote this celebratory obituary for her:

A Nonagenarian Remembered

In memory of Irene Ann Heredia
22 September 1917–21 January 2013

You rarely called me,
It's I who called you every day and more
just to break the silent stillness
of your long day and cheer you for the morrow,
so you'd have something to wake up for
each time you go to rest.

But when you would call me
It would always be to ask after me
and whether I was taking good care of myself.

So when you rang me that morning on the train
to tell me you weren't too well and
that I wouldn't be hearing from you in a while,
I sensed it was the end game now
and I was left hoping, praying
I'd be there for you before it was over and out.

Gradually as it sank in
I found myself feeling
so intensely proud of you
and your journey on your long way home,
for all you've been and mean
to me and so many on whom you left
your gentle imprint.

The empty space you'll leave behind
will be too large to fill;
it will remain an aching longing
at the end of each long day

I'll miss you in my emptiness
left to wait and to remember,
feel proud and happy over and again
Your remembrance will lift and heal,
and float the hearts of those
you once reached out to
and now have left behind.

Memories and nostalgia are
all that's left to unite us now.
But when the kingdom comes
We'll once again relive those days
of long ago and far away,
familiar still for our having shared them once
and now so easy to recall yet once again.

Be no longer anxious, woman,
though it's been a very long day.
May our sunsets now light up our eyes
to see the stars awaiting for the dawn,
the sunrise of another day,
in some other place,
a new heaven and a new earth,
where every tear will be wiped from every eye,
and death shall be no more.

And all that was so lovely and precious,
so beautiful and wonderful,
will last forever in the new life
that banishes forever
the darkness in our souls.

God be with you gentle woman
to light your way,
and may angels guide to your new home.

But we're walking close behind,
so that the promises we shared together will
fulfil the promise that we are and called to be,
to one another and to oneself, together.

(21 January 2013)

DISPARATE COMMUNITY

Back at Campion, I began working on my third book again. I cannot say the community was a help though it wasn't too much of a hindrance either. It was quite a disparate community: four Jesuits doing different things with little to unite them. Over the four years I was there, the superior kept asking me to support myself and earn my per diem. The province would pay, I said, if the community couldn't afford me. But he wouldn't say that, because the province treasurer would have challenged him on it.

Finally, I had to ask the Provincial to intervene and put things right but the nagging didn't stop. Money only talks to such men, everything else is silenced. So now I ended up feeling like an un-paying guest. He once actually said to me: writing is so easy; just sit in front of a computer and type. How would he know when he's hardly written anything! But then neither did Socrates. This similarity is purely accidental!

I took a break in 2014 on a fellowship being offered to a Jesuit from the developing countries by St Louis University, Missouri USA. I opted to stay with the scholastics at Bellarmine House in St Louis, Missouri, USA. It was a very positive learning experience for me, living with young Jesuits, and getting to know some inspiring superiors, Ron Mercier and Doug Marcouiller. I was grateful for the chance to spend time in the library and catch up on my reading for the next book I was working on—*Reconciling Difference: Collective Violence in India*. And even to touch base with some old friends from an earlier time in another space. With such old friends, it is like picking up the conversation where we left the last time we had met long years ago.

THIRD AVATAR AT ISI

But that was only a stop-gap. I realized that I would have to break out of Campion to a place that had more positive energy. So I wrote to the Director of ISI, Fr Denzil Fernandes, to ask if there was room for me. He wrote back, inviting me to join them. I asked him to work out the details of the appointment. He created a new post, 'Research Consultant', a term which sometimes confused people.

'What's that?' they'd ask. I'd reply, 'I don't quite know and don't want to either; the ambiguity suits me!'

So my third avatar began on a sober note in 2016 with a few summary reviews and evaluations of apostolic works and working on papers the POSA asked me to do. I attended some conferences and seminars at which I presented papers and gave some inaugural lectures. It ended on a high note in 2020. I worked in an isolated office on the first floor at the end of a corridor. It had windows opening to the green lawn of the Institute's garden, very different from the basement office I had earlier, which had only a skylight ventilator to let in some fresh air.

In the new office I finished the third book I was working on *Reconciling Difference: Collective Violence in India* (Speaking Tiger, 2021). I felt appreciated and trusted by the Jesuit community and the Institute staff, and I wanted to respond to their confidence and trust to the best of my ability. After all for confidence and trust to last it must be reciprocal.

I leaned on the support I got from each one and they all stood by me and facilitated my work and my research in spite of my health issues which got me into hospital with hypertension and related illnesses a couple of times during my stint in Delhi. I am so grateful to the community, the administrator, Fr Shiju, and especially the superior, Fr Joy Karayapuram, one of the best superiors I've had. He returned to his province, Patna, in 2020 as Rector of St Xavier's College there. Most tragically, he fell a victim to Covid-19 in 2021. It was a very personal loss to many of us, especially me.

But I am happy to report that these last few years have been a smooth ride thanks to their community care and the concern of each member, the wonderful superiors who believed in the intellectual apostolate, and have wiped out the trust deficit precipitated by the some earlier ones, who were so much out of their depth, clowns without humour. Here I had real role models: caring, understanding superiors, a Director with a creative vision for the institute, a very proactive administrator, and even a caring chef, an obliging faculty and staff, and the several related units and centres which were housed under the same roof. And of course many friends and soul mates in the city.

I was the oldest in the Jesuit community and they treated me as an elder brother. If had stayed on longer I might have graduated to 'grandfather'. I was not ready for that as yet!

MOVING ON

I returned to Xavier's after sixteen years to find the community had changed completely. The old guard had fallen out with each other and had moved on, or been moved out and replaced by a new cadre, mostly elderly and retired men whom time had left behind. The Jesuit community was now drastically depleted and the imperative of collaboration had finally caught up with us. The college now has a non-Catholic principal, who seemed to fit into the shoes of his office quite comfortably. The old Jesuit community has been reduced to a remnant, ageing, tired and over stretched. There were just seven Jesuits in the community: three in their eighties, just two younger men, one a scholastic still in training while teaching, another away in tertianship. The Rector was gallantly trying to put together a team including laypersons. But as a Jesuit community they seem unable and/or unwilling to take on the additional responsibility for such care as an ailing Jesuit might need.

The few able Jesuits were already over stretched. However, instead of accommodating and adjusting to new personnel, many of the older Jesuits were turning inward. This would inevitably mean writing their own epitaph and it isn't likely to be a happy one. What was once the largest apostolic community in our province and a very dynamic one had been reduced to a mere half dozen Jesuits with just a couple below the age of retirement.

Rather than swim with this receding tide over mud flats, I thought I'd save what energies I have left for another monograph, *Tolerating the Intolerable: Piety and Prejudice in India.* I may not get that far but at least I'll have put together this memoir, *A Clown for God.* I have also begun working on my old papers, editing and sorting them out into intelligible volumes, with help from old and faithful friends. And it's been a yeoman ask.

A MIX OF CLOWNS

There are many clowns reflected and refracted in this 'tale told in a minor chord': some good, some bad, some quite mad, some rather sad. The teller of the tale is happy to be a mix of many such clowns and maybe more. Little wonder then that his identity is often mistaken and misrecognized. But genuine clowns are comfortable with that as long as their real identity is not hidden from themselves. Living in a make-believe world only impoverishes, rather than enriches, our real personal one.

Arrupe Niwas, named after Father Pedro Arrupe, in St Mary's High School, Mazagaon, is a Jesuit residence designed for assisted care. Here, I feel well taken care of and fairly secure. I still have my mind, my friends, my books, my notes and I'm able to keep writing—at least so far. Now in my eightieth year, I'm the second youngest in the Niwas. Only I do feel that what the

Niwas needs is a concerned carer, rather than a directing administrator; an imaginative overseer rather than an over-cautious supervisor. Often those living in such residences are more in need of *concerned human caring* than *professional medical assistance*, for it is human contact and engagement, humane touch and reassurance that is the most healing and wholesome remedy for their difficult predicament.

MISTAKEN IDENTITY

This tale told by a clown is best symbolized by the confusion created by someone who reported that Fr Rudy was down with COVID-19 in the Nashik Civil Hospital's ICU. I started getting phone calls to verify where I was and the callers wouldn't believe I was in Mumbai. So when an official notification came out announcing Fr Rudy's demise in the hospital, I decided I had to send out a missive of my own as evidence I was still on earth, not in heaven or hell, or even purgatory. It was just a case of mistaken identity between Rud*y* Fernandes, a gentle saint, and Rud*i* Heredia, a discomforter of the comfortable but sometimes perhaps a comforter of the discomfited too.

I wouldn't put it down to a Freudian slip or wish because the confusion had happened before. Taking a group of sociology students on a weekend fieldtrip to Nashik, I was alarmed to be told there was a woman on the platform demanding to meet Fr Rudi. It turned out this was a genuine mistake and no mischief was being blamed on anyone! I wasn't the Rudi she was looking for, it was the other Fr Rudy Fernandes.

LIVING INTENSELY

From where I'm at now, I do feel God's providence ruling my life. There but for the grace of God go I.

Look Back in Wonder

In the rush and tumble of my life,
I look with gratitude and find
the things that accidently happened,
on the paths I chose, or were imposed,
when some doors opened and others closed.

And I wonder at the providence that rules my life
through all the ups and downs, the highs and lows,
constraints from outside, and from within.
Some brought joy, and others grief,
but yet I get by with a little help from my friends.

Now I look forward in hope
to a future crashing in on me
and in gratitude and hope,
I seize the present moment gifted to my care.

Then with trusting faith,
I walk my talk with blistered feet,
pick up with my bleeding hands
the burden of my unresolved forgiveness
with a grateful, faithful, hopeful heart.

(15 July 2017)

I have also known the pain of a desolate devotee longing for an:

Absent God

I've searched so long for you,
or was it really an eternity? I'll never know.
So what's a decade or two yet again
to lose and find you once more forever?

And you, my truant teacher,
my ever-restless pilgrim deity,
will you turn away to other devotees
and never wait for me?

I've harvested the moonlight
with my bare hands for your delight,
and moved the mountains with my faith
to lay them in devotion at your feet!

I've sought the rarest flowers
in my desert wilderness
yet always found your beauty,
still incomparable,
ever ancient, ever new!

Now with bruised hands
and broken hopes
the blood still dried upon my face
my soul lies buried under
an avalanche of despair.

Late have I loved thee
'O beauty ever ancient, ever new',
but what's a maya of desolation
for that moment of truth
with you in mystic ecstasy forever?

(July 1999)

I have always wanted to live an intense life, one that would combine total commitment with complete detachment. But I did not give enough importance to the backlash that critical truth-telling precipitates, especially when this questions the status quo or the comfort zones of others, and more so when it goes without any compassionate healing. In my arrogance, I was dismissive of the negative feedback I got: 'If they can't cope, well then that's their problem not mine.' I'm wiser now: critique, however insightful, must be compassionate; and truth-telling however objective must be healing.

To live intensely, we must live transparent to our own self and others, that is to be honest. This is more than being merely sincere, which implies consistency between what we mean and what we express, internally to oneself and externally to the other. Honesty is about transparency and openness, sincerity is about feeling and expression. Thus an angry person expressing anger, rather than equivocating it, is sincere. But neglecting to probe its underlying causes is not being self-transparent, not being honest with oneself. And then how can one begin to be honest with others.

Authentic, humanizing intensity demands both honesty and sincerity, or else it only adds up to mere feverish excitement or some melodramatic excess. Either of these tip over into taking oneself over-seriously and being dismissive of others. Thus it queers the pitch for all concerned and we are likely to end up in the rat-race only to become rats ourselves. We get into the fast track and eventually crash out in some unforeseen disaster travelling.

Fast Forward

Hurtling down the fast track
in overdrive mode,
the video dismembers the scene
into endless shapes,
the images squirm
and squeeze themselves
into formlessness;
the audio squeaks,
the words spit and cough,
in rasping lisps.

Rioting colours, streaking around,
splashing light, crashing sounds,
spasms and orgies, the quiet of night,
premature burn out, flaccid flight.

The world whistles by
with doppler effects,
yet all the while
in open country scenes
life seems staid, stilled.

And suddenly
a switch trips, the power cuts,
a screech, a crash,
the rhythm's broken, the tape snaps,
the airbags explode, the seatbelts lock,
the swish-swosh spinning
of arrhythmic mime,
strobe light flashes, black on white,
the radio survives with the nine o'clock news.

The rest is silence, all is darkness.
At a dead-end now,
lost, aching, waiting, wanting
a more gentle redemption
for the remains of the day!
Who will be there?
When it's too late?
And night?

(July 1999)

A TALE TOLD IN A MINOR KEY

Clowns find their joy in the laughter of others. They choose to expose their vulnerability to help others cope. And the more decisive they are about this, the more convincing they become. This is the blessed that means 'happy'. This is the blessedness, the beatitudes, that must add up to in these troubled times: a sustained and consistent endeavour towards a counter-culture for the common good, not selfish greed.

Of course, there are unfortunately bad clowns too. But this, I believe, generally comes of weakness, which they struggle to cover up and hide. We don't have to humour them, but we must at all times deal even with bad clowns and worse, with good humour.

However, it requires an emotional intelligence to situate a text in its context, an action in its sitz-im-leben and grasp what is being communicated. Sometimes it runs counter to what is being said or done. Focusing on feelings opens the communication to better understanding; analyzing it often leads to misunderstanding or worse, closure. The genius of the clowns is to understand with their hearts rather than their heads. But at times clowns too can miss the point and lose the plot for being too preoccupied elsewhere.

So those bright young things who waited after class to tell me they felt sorry for me? If they really did, they wouldn't have waited to tell me. Only later I realized when they became my friends and not just my students, that they were trying to open up a conversation beyond the sociology classroom. Or that the seventeen-year-old who had the temerity to throw my books out of window, was trying to get my attention to which, as a student, she felt she had a claim on and more so, when she became my friend.

On another more dramatic occasion a student stormed into my office with: 'The trouble with you is that you don't know all the girls who are in love with you!' I shrugged nonchalantly thinking that may not be such a good thing for a teacher. She went on with: 'And worse you don't know the girls whom you are in love with!' This was more serious. So I collected myself and replied: 'And whom may I ask are you in love with?' At which she stormed out of my office with: 'You stupid man!' I should have realized that she was making a difficult transference from treating me as a respected teacher to being a good and loving friend. Eventually, we did become lasting friends and could laugh over the incident. I still tease her about needing a 'Vico Vajradanti' mouth wash to stop bad-mouthing me.

There have been occasions when my feedback, asked for and sincerely and honestly given, has precipitated such a stormy negative response, an explosion that frightened me into withdrawal. It was only when I realized that my feedback had touched a raw nerve and the angry response was not a rejection but a cry for help, could I respond more positively and affectionately, building new bridges, healing old hurt.

At times I have felt so close to someone that I have thought my love was too obvious to need my expressing it, as with my dad and mom. I could only write about my feelings for them after they were gone and I had come to terms with their departure (as with 'Unfinished Farewells', and 'A Nonagenarian Remembered').

So now I ask my friends and companions—who have crossed the bar before me to be my guardian angels here—as symbolized in this farewell to Adrian, my Jesuit friend who walked many a venture with me, as have others—too many to mention here Jesuits and non-Jesuits, men and women, friends and soul mates. I hope to catch up with them all in the resurrection, which is already now, but not fully yet:

Farewell for a Soul Mate

Adrian D'Cruz, S.J
(26 March 1939–4 September 2017)

On my road to Emmaus
I'm so grateful I met you
and you shared yourself with me.
I'm even more grateful you accepted me

and what I shared with you.
We found each other in our broken lives,
in breaking bread together,
climbing hill tops, staring down
the valleys into the dark below,
redeeming broken promises,
healing wounded lives,
as we journeyed onward to Jerusalem
on untrod paths that sometimes parted,
sometimes met and crossed and merged,
yet always pointed to that city on the hill,
where promises are fulfilled and dreams come true.

Now you're home on top, where you belong
I'm on the way, I'm almost there.
Be my guardian angel, strong Adrian,
till I am home.

(8 September 2017)

I could say as much of many of my Jesuit friends in the lord and companions on missions, and so many other men and women. For in the final analysis, I belong to the Society of Jesus, its vision and mission, not so much by the structures that bind me to it, but through the network of interpersonal relationships I have with the friends and companions that bind me to this band of brothers and sisters, this Jesuit family, to all who have touched my heart, and lightened my way.

A Blessing

May the promises hidden deep in your heart
fulfil the person you were meant to be.
May the paths you choose in life

open to enchanting scenes.
May your fellow-travellers
be companions on your journey
to a brave new world.
May the dreams your dream
awaken you to beautiful days.
May the friends you make
be yours for keeps.
May you meet with soul mates
on your way
to enrich each other's lives forever.
As you have mine.

(14 July 2017)

ORGANIZATION TRIAGE AND LIFE CYCLE

Triage is common to any organization: a third of the members at the leading edge; a third make up those who let things get done and manage to get by; and there are a third who must be carried through the heat and burden of the day.

I have known many heroic Jesuits and others, exemplars who have been challenging role models for me. I still pray at their graves at Vinayalaya when I can. The trailing third in the Society are not employees who can be dismissed; they are volunteers who must be persuasively re-motivated. I have seen many a transformation here too. And the middle third? They too are fellow-travellers who sometimes settle into comfort zones but who can also rise to meet a challenge. I have seen Kalinga moments like Ashoka's, or conversions like Paul's on the road to Damascus. I have seen scriptures transforming despairing hearts on the road to Emmaus, and heard of many renunciates who were once dacoits. Miracles make life liveable; and they happen much more frequently than we would imagine.

Moreover, this is part of an organization's life cycle, and more so that of individual persons as well. Only a constant return to the original charism keeps the vision and mission bright and burning, and the love story moving forward for new and wonderful things to happen. For Jesuits it is the Jesus myth. As Fr Pedro Arrupe put it, a personal love for the person of Jesus, the saviour-myth that is ever ancient and ever new, of which we sometimes learn too late.

TRAVELLING TOGETHER

Too often, in too many lives, the future crashes into them, bringing shock and trauma. I would rather walk into the future hoping I will be remembered for the good I did and the difference it made, knowing too I am forgiven by the people I've hurt and the harm I've done has healed. 'Clowning' has been a metaphor I have used for this journey, of many little 'deaths' but far more and greater 'resurrections'.

The appreciation of the comic in our lives serves as a much-needed corrective to taking ourselves over-seriously, and forgetting the ever present 'circus-like' world we inhabit. Royal courts had their 'jesters', as Akbar had Birbal. So why not a clown in the religious courtyards of the Jesuits, and the ecclesial ones of the Church?

Clowns help us see that 'all the world's a stage', we all have our entrances and exits; and in between we play many parts, which add up to the complex story of our lives. Clowns bring with them much-needed healing laughter and relativizing humour to the ups and downs of our journey. They help us capture the nostalgia of the past with gratitude and to open for us a future of hope with joy. So it's never too late to 'call in the clowns', indeed there ought to be clowns; if only we'd look, already they're here.

The 'clown' calls us to travel together, like a performing circus, forming 'community' on the way, intertwining our lives as we begin birthing a future still known. The future is born in the past, lies hidden in the present, and remains an invitation to reach out to receding horizons and float beyond them over the rainbow to a land we once dreamt of in lullabies of bygone days and faraway places. But it is a future we can't control. And so we are:

Floating on Hope

As we walk together for a while,
we could become companions along the way
bound together heart to heart
soul-mates on a pilgrimage
floating on a hope for a better

more beautiful, more compassionate world
for tomorrow and beyond,
for ourselves and others
and every single one.

(10 April 2013)

WALKING INTO THE FUTURE

I want to walk into my future not as a settler in a comfort zone, but rather one who comforts the discomforted and discomforts the comfortable as John Kenneth Galbraith once challenged young graduates at their 'commencement'. But on this pilgrimage I could well become a scapegoat, the 'homo sacer' of Giorgio Agamben, sacrificed by his people for communal peace, though I'd rather be a 'homo ambulans', critical of the establishment, the status quo, trying to *be* constructive even at the risk of *being seen* as hyper-critical, rather than helpfully positive, hopefully not cynical but creative. If I can't be them, never joining them opportunistically but striving to remain, not the last man standing, but the one still walking into the future. For I believe this earth was meant for us to walk on, not lie under, not until our cue calls us to exit the stage set for us.

Here then is my image of this:

Homo Ambulans

I want to walk this earth as Jesus did,
making a difference,
bringing wholeness and healing

to a bruised and broken world,
helping to fulfil the hidden promises
deep in people's hearts;
walking with friends and companions,
with soul mates and fellow-travellers,
with wayfarers and wanderers on the way.

And when I must,
walking alone with my absent-God,
echoing in my heart Tagore's haunting song
Êkla Chôlo Re, Êkla Chôlo Re
(Walk Alone, Walk Alone),
but always and everywhere
walking with hope, daring the future,
which is already now but not fully yet.
Walk me into your future, O my God!

Wayfarer, will you walk with me and be
a friend, companion, soul-mate and mentor?

(3 June 2017)

THE CIRCUS OF LIFE

I must recognize in gratitude the numerous friends and companions who have accompanied me on the circus of my life; Jesuits and friends, family and relatives, men and women, young and old, students and teachers, beautiful persons, and not quite to lovable ones...too many to be mentioned here by name. I do certainly hold them in my heart, remembering the good times, the cheer and laughter we shared along the way over the years; as also the less memorable instances of jeers and sneers; all of these and more that have been valuable learning experiences for me. They have all contributed to what I am today.

Over the years our paths would meet and sync, and at times cross and part. However, despite the differences and disagreements, which would at times set us off on alternative journeys, there was far more we shared, as we impacted each other's lives, in a dialogue of word and action, in prayer and silence. For no matter how great the distance between us, there was always that inclusion in a larger quest, in a not always fully articulated pursuit of both: the commitment to the more inclusive common good of all, however that is ultimately defined; as well as the search for that deeper intimacy with the transcendent mystery of life, or by whichever one of the many names it is called.

For in these shared relationships with my 'soulmates', as I call them, of intimacy and mystery, I will always treasure the ways in which they have marked my life making it the more beautiful and precious. I hope the gift they have been to me has been reciprocated in some measure.

Of course, no life-journey can be entirely devoid of misunderstanding and hurt, yet when healing and restoration comes with forgiveness and pardon, our love is twice as precious for having lost for a little while, only to be found again more enriched.

There are many clowns in this memoir but only one ring master for the circus, the Providence that rules all our lives. Some of my soulmates have crossed the bar into the beyond; others are still walking with me, sometimes together, sometimes alone, but always into a newness of life that begins already now but not fully yet. Where, as TS Eliot opined in 'Little Gidding':

> We shall not cease from exploration
> And the end of all our exploring
> Will be to arrive where we started
> And know the place for the first time.

I await this future 'with a great curiosity' as John Henry Newman did. For the best is yet to come, in the resurrection, the qayamat, with nirvana, moksha, where God will be all in all, and we will be God's one people; 'where all things will be well, all things will be very well' (Juliana of Norwich).

ENVOI

Every parting is a little death, but it can also be a bigger resurrection. This is tantamount to me saying: I'm sorry to leave but I'm happy to go. I suspect that this is because one does not want to feel the parting is a loss of the old, but a gain with the new that is born thereafter. The first is a little death, the second a greater resurrection. This is the death-resurrection mystery enacted in our lives. I believe that these little deaths in our life's journey will add up in the end, to the final 'Resurrection', the 'Qayamat' of the Quran, like Moksha of the Upanishads, the Nirvana of the Buddha.

The joy of this 'resurrection' is really the faith that everything good, beautiful, precious and lovely in our lives will never be lost; that all the people we have loved, the bonds we have forged, the experiences we treasure, the relationships that have made us, all this and more is carried over into the kingdom of God which begins already now but is not fully yet. For the future is but the noumenon of the present phenomena. These may distort our perception of the deeper reality, but once unmasked they can never suppress the future hope hidden therein.

And so I end for now as always with this:

Prayer

May your hope lift you up
against all hopelessness.
May your love bring you ecstasy,
even as you root your feet
firmly to walk this earth
in joy and freedom
in hope and compassion,
for yourself and others.

(19 April 2021)

ACKNOWLEDGEMENTS

My gratitude to Jerry, my literary mentor and guide, friend and critic, for bringing closure to this monograph which just might have turned into an endless polygraph. Also for the support of the Aruppe Niwas and St Mary's community and Fr Jude Fernandes; as well as to my publisher, Ravi Singh, of Speaking Tiger, and Radhika Shenoy, the copy editor. And of course, to the many other players (and clowns!) in this tale (circus!).